RIVER
THAMES

GW00371906

VANESSA LETTS

WESTMINSTER MILLENNIUM PIER - ST KATHARINE'S PIER - BARRIER GARDENS PIER (Thames Barrier) (TC)

Cruise time: 1 hour 10 mins.
Operator: Thames Cruises,
(020) 7930 3373.

EMBANKMENT PIER - TOWER MILLENNIUM PIER - ST KATHARINE'S PIER - GREENWICH PIER (CAT)

Cruise time: 1 hour.
Operator: Catamaran Cruises,
(020) 7987 1185,
www.catamarancruises.co.uk

CH PIER – BARRIER GARDENS PIER (Thames Barrier) GREENWICH PIER (CL)

Cruise time: 30 mins, return 1 hour.
Operator: Campion Launches,
(020)8305 0300.

Upstream (westbound) riverboat services

WESTMINSTER MILLENNIUM PIER - KEW PIER - RICHMOND PIER - HAMPTON COURT PIER (WU)

The timetable is subject to alteration at short notice owing to extreme tidal conditions between Kew and Hampton Court: always phone ahead. No service 30 October – 1 April.
Cruise time: 3 hours 30 mins. Return trip: 7–8 hours.
Operator: Westminster Passenger Service Association,
(020) 7930 2062/4721,
www.wpsa.co.uk

Circular Cruises

FROM WATERLOO MILLENNIUM PIER and EMBANKMENT PIER (CAT)

Cruise time: 50 mins.
Operator: Catamaran Cruises,
(020) 7987 1185,
www.catamarancruises.co.uk
Live commentary in seven languages.

Up and downstream Commuter Services (Mon–Fri only)

SAVOY PIER - BLACKFRIARS MILLENNIUM PIER - LONDON BRIDGE CITY PIER - ST KATHARINE'S PIER - CANARY WHARF PIER - HOLIDAY INN ROTHERHITHE PIER - GREENLAND PIER (CE)

Early morning and afternoon commuter service.
Sailing time: every 25 mins.
Operator: Collins River Enterprises,
(020) 7237 9538,
www.thamescat.com

CADOGAN PIER - WESTMINSTER MILLENNIUM PIER - BLACKFRIARS MILLENNIUM PIER (TS)

Every 30 mins from 7am–7pm or later; single fare from £1.80.

Sailing time: Every 25 mins.
Operator: Thames Speed Ferry Company,
(020) 7731 7671,
www.thamesferry.com

Lunch Cruises

THE SILVER BONITO (WO)

Leaves from Embankment Pier passing the Houses of Parliament, The Tower of London and the Dome. Ticket (around £17) includes three course 'airline' meal, wine and commentary.
Cruise time: 2 hours.
Operator: Woods River Cruises,
(020) 7480 7770,
www.woodsrivercruises.com

BATEAUX LONDON LUNCH CRUISE (BAL)

Leaves from Embankment Pier passing the Houses of Parliament, The Tower of London and the Dome. Tickets (£20-28) include three course meal.
Cruise time: 1 or 2 hours.
Operator: Bateaux London,
(020) 7925 2215,
www.bateauxlondon.com

Dinner Cruises

LONDON SHOWBOAT DINNER CRUISE (CY)

Leaves from Westminster Millennium Pier passing the Houses of Parliament, The Tower of London and the Dome. Tickets (around £45) include a four course supper with wine and a live cabaret and disco.
Cruise time: 3.5 hours.
Operator: City Cruises,
(020) 7237 5134,
www.citycruises.com

BATEAUX LONDON DINNER CRUISE (BAL)

Leaves from Embankment Pier passing the Houses of Parliament, The Tower of London and the Dome. Tickets (£57-70) include four course meal, wine and cabaret and after dinner dancing.
Cruise time: 3.5 hours.
Operator: Bateaux London,
(020) 7925 2215,
www.bateauxlondon.com

Boats for hire

Transport for London (see p7 above) can provide a complete list.
Campion, (020) 8305 0300.
Colliers Launches, (020) 8892 0741.
Paddle Steamer Kingswear Castle Trust, (01634) 827648.
Steamship Streatley, (01628) 474047.
Thames Luxury Charters, (020) 8780 1562.
Westminster Park Boats, (020) 7839 3424.

River Map

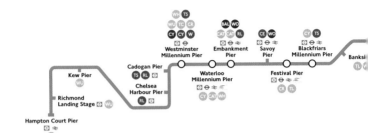

Key to symbols

● Luncheon/Dinner Cruise

● Direct Cruise

● Commuter Service

● Leisure Cruise

● Circular Cruise

● Central London Fast Ferry

ᴅʟʀ Docklands Light Railway connections

⊖ Bus connections

⊖ Underground connections

⇌ National Railway connections within walking distance

⇌ Eurostar interchange

○ Interchange stations

W Woolwich Free Ferry

Frog Tours

The circular non stopping route starts at County Hall, crossing Westminster Bridge and then continues via Parliament Square, Whitehall, Trafalgar Square, Piccadilly, Hyde Park Corner, Buckingham Palace, Victoria and Vauxhall Bridge, This tour only takes 80 minutes. **Frogs 'Splashdown' into the Thames at Lacks Dock Vauxhall and the river element lasts approximately 30 minutes with the Frogs travelling down river to turn round in front of The London Eye, (Millennium Wheel).** On leaving the river, Frogs return to County Hall via the Embankment passing Lambeth Palace along the south bank of the Thames.

The London Frog Company
County Hall
Westminster Bridge Road
London SE1 7PB
Tel: 020 7928 6162
Booking line: 020 7928 3132

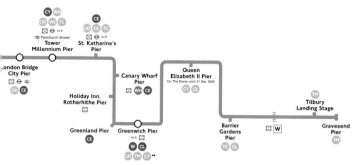

Key to routes and operators

RL Chelsea - Embankment
Riverside Launches

WU Westminster - Hampton Court
Westminster Passenger Service Association (Upriver)

CY Westminster - Tower
City Cruises

CY London Showboat Dinner Cruise
City Cruises

TC Westminster - Thames Barrier
Thames Cruises

W Westminster - Greenwich
Westminster Passenger Services

CR Westminster - St. Katharine's
- Westminster
Crown River Cruises

TP Westminster Circular Cruises
Thames Pleasure Cruises

BAL Embankment
Bateaux London Restaurant Cruises

CAT Embankment - Greenwich
Catamaran Cruisers

CAT Multi-lingual Circular Cruises
Catamaran Cruisers

WO Silver Fleet Dinner/Luncheon Cruise
Woods River Cruises

TL Tower - Festival - Bankside
Thames Leisure

WH Blackfriars - Rotherhithe
White Horse Fast Ferries

CE Savoy - Greenland
Collins River Enterprises

WE Balmoral and Waverley at Tower Pier
Waverley Excursions

CL Greenwich Sunday Evening Cruise
Campion Launches

CL Greenwich - Thames Barrier
Campion Launches

WH Greenwich - Dome Shuttle
White Horse Fast Ferries

CY Millennium Express
City Cruises

TM Gravesend/Tilbury - Greenwich
Lower Thames & Medway Passenger
Boat Company

11

HAMPTON COURT

East Molesey, Surrey, (020) 8781 9500,
Website: www.hrp.org.uk
Open: Apr–Nov, Tues–Sun 9.30–6, Mon 10.15–6; Nov–Apr, Tues–Sun
9.30–4.30, Mon 10.15–4.30.
Admission: £10.50, family ticket £31.40, concs £8, 5s-15s £7.
Transport: Riverboat to Hampton Court

Like many a bouquet of flowers, Hampton Court was a peace offering. Cardinal Wolsey bought the site in 1514 and by the time he gave it to Henry VIII, some twelve years later, he had created one of the grandest country palaces in England, with 280 guest rooms, a retinue of 500 servants, several moats and

custom-built sewers. Henry accepted the gift gladly enough and then, when Wolsey failed to secure him a divorce from Catherine of Aragon, had him arrested for high treason. Wolsey died in transit to the Tower of London.

Five of Henry's wives were brought to live in Hampton Court: Anne Boleyn lasted three years before she was executed at the Tower; Jane Seymour, who died twelve days after giving birth to Henry's heir, is supposed to haunt the queen's apartments, dressed in white and carrying a taper; Catherine Howard, beheaded 18 months after she became queen, still stalks the Haunted Gallery. Henry's most enduring love affair was with Hampton Court itself and he lavished money on it, adding a Great Hall, a real tennis court, vast kitchens and an astronomical clock in which the sun travels around the earth.

When William and Mary came to live in Hampton Court in 1688 they recruited Christopher Wren to transform it into a second Versailles. Only part of the scheme was completed, and Hampton Court's handsome riverside façade remains as it was in Tudor times. William decorated the new apartments with paintings by Verrio, Gobelin tapestries from Brussels and Delftware from Holland, restored the phenomenal *Mantegna Triumphs of Caesar*, and redesigned the gardens, adding a herb garden and the famous maze.

KINGSTON BRIDGE

Jerome K. Jerome kept his boat at Kingston, and Kingston Bridge was the starting point for the river journey to Oxford described in his novel *Three Men in a Boat*. A stone bridge was built across this point as early as 1170; Kingston itself is one of the four oldest royal boroughs, and a prehistoric stone outside the Guildhall is thought to be the Coronation stone on which seven Anglo-Saxon kings were crowned.

FOOD AND DRINK

The Boaters Inn

Lower Ham Road, Kingston-Upon-Thames, Surrey,
(020) 8541 4672.
Open: all day Apr-Sep.Food served: daily 12–2.30, 7–9.30.

Situated on a rural stretch of the river between Teddington Lock and Kingston, this excellent rowing club pub has its own outdoor drinking deck and garden.

The Tide End Cottage

8-10 Ferry Road, Teddington, (020) 8977 7762.
Open: Food served: Mon-Sat 12–2.30, 6–9, Sun 12–5, 6–8.

Victorian fisherman's cottage next to Teddington Lock

STRAWBERRY HILL

to arrange a private tour (020) 8240 4114.

This eccentric building was the creation of Horace Walpole, the father of the English 'Gothick' Novel. Walpole bought the coachman's cottage in 1747 ('so small I can send it you in a letter to look at'), renamed it Strawberry Hill and spent the next 50 years transforming it into a baronial castle. Tombs, cloisters and ruined abbeys were lovingly copied and remodelled. The papier-maché fan-vaulted ceiling in the Long Gallery comes from Henry VII's chapel at

Westminster Abbey; the Round Room fireplace was an 'improved' Edward the Confessor's tomb. Walpole even invented a bogus ancestor – Sir Terry Robsart who had been in the Crusades – and embellished the library ceiling with his initials. By the 1760s Strawberry Hill had become a tourist attraction; Walpole printed entrance tickets and received visitors dressed in a lavender suit and silver waistcoat. It was Strawberry Hill, finally, which inspired Walpole's Gothic extravaganza The *Castle of Otranto*, written in 60 days after Walpole dreamt of a gigantic armoured hand dangling over his staircase.

FOOD AND DRINK

The White Swan,

Riverside, Twickenham, (020) 8892 2166.
Food served: daily 12–2.30, Mon–Thur 7-9.

This lovely Twickenham pub dates from the 1690s and has a three-cornered room and balcony overlooking the river.

ORLEANS HOUSE GALLERY

Riverside, Twickenham, (020) 8892 0221.
Open: Apr–Sep, Tues–Sat 1–5.30, Sun 2–5.30; Oct–Mar,
Tues-Sat 1–4.30, Sun 2–4.30.
Admission: free.
Transport: train to St Margaret's.

The name commemorates the Duke of Orléans, later restored as King Louis Philippe, who fled the French Revolution to live in exile here from 1800–17. In 1927 nearly all the building was demolished except for James Gibbs' turret-like Octagon Room which was saved at the last minute and is now an art gallery showing a varied programme of contemporary and historical art.

MARBLE HILL HOUSE

Richmond Road, Twickenham, (020) 8892 5115.
Open: Apr–Sept, daily 10–6; Oct–Mar, Wed–Sun 10–4.
Admission: £3, concs £2.30, 5s-15s £1.50.
Transport: train/tube to Richmond.

This immaculately restored Palladian villa was built for George II's mistress, Henrietta Howard. It was a bolt-hole from the pressures of life at Court and became a regular meeting place for the writers and poets Horace Walpole, Jonathan Swift, John Gay and Alexander Pope (who lived next door).

Marble Hill Festival: In July and August there are concerts beside the river in Marble Hill Park, (020) 8223 for information and box office (020) 7344 4444.

RICHMOND BRIDGE & LOCK

When old London Bridge was demolished in 1832, the usual tidal flows altered and this stretch of the Thames shrank to little more than a trickle. After protests from residents a retractable dam was built to keep water levels high at low tide. Built in 1777, Richmond Bridge is London's oldest surviving bridge and the one that inspired Wordsworth's lines:

> *Glide gently, thus for ever glide*
> *O Thames! that other bards may see*
> *As lovely visions by thy side*
> *As now, fair river! come to me.*

FOOD AND DRINK

The Waterman's Arms

12 Water Lane, Richmond, (020) 8940 2893.
Food served: daily 12–2.30.

This venerable pub on the southeast side of Richmond Bridge dates from 1660: traditionally the Swan Uppers stopped here for lunch on their way from Blackfriars to Henley.

The White Cross

Riverside, Richmond, (020) 8940 6844.
Food served: daily 12–4.

Large and atmospheric early Victorian pub with open fires.

RICHMOND DEER PARK
Richmond, Surrey, (020) 8948 3209.
Open: Mar-Sep, daily 7-dusk; Oct-Feb, daily 7.30-dusk. Admission: free.
Transport: train or tube to Richmond then 371 bus.

At 2,500 acres, Richmond is London's largest and wildest park. Though sovereigns used the area for hunting deer since medieval times, Charles I went one step further and, in 1637, enclosed it in an 8-mile brick wall. In 1751 the wall was smashed down and the deer chase was handed back. These days its unspoiled tracts of grass, wetland, bracken and ancient oak woods are home to hares, rabbits, weasels and 700 fallow and red deer, so many that there has to be an annual cull.

SYON HOUSE & GARDENS
Brentford, Middlesex, ∞ (020) 8560 0881.
Open: house open Apr–Oct, Wed–Thurs & Sun 11–5; gardens open daily 10-dusk.
Admission: to both £6, family ticket £15, concs and 5s-15s £4.50; gardens only £3, concs and 5s-15s £2.50.
Transport: tube to Gunnersbury; train to Kew Bridge.

Syon House's many attractions include a trout fishery, an aquarium, an indoor adventure playground, a miniature steam railway, a garden centre and the London Butterfly House, home to butterflies and moths from every continent. The house itself has a darker history: originally an abbey, it was seized by Henry VIII who incarcerated Catherine Howard within it shortly before her beheading in 1542. A friar spoke menacingly of dogs licking the king's blood in divine retribution, a prophesy that came true when Henry VIII's funeral cortège stopped at Syon on its way to Windsor and the next morning the servants found a burst-open coffin and pack of hounds gobbling up the King's remains.

The house was given to the Percys in 1600 and remains in the family. In the 1760s it was transformed by Robert Adam and Capability Brown, who remodelled all the interiors and landscaped the grounds, adding vistas and two lakes. One of Syon's finest buildings (now a garden centre) is the Bath stone Great Conservatory designed in the 1820s by Charles Fowler and the inspiration for Joseph Paxton's Crystal Palace.

KEW GARDENS

(020) 8332 5000, recorded info (020) 8940 1171, www.kew.org
Open: daily 9.30–dusk.
Admission: £5, concs £3.50, 5s-15s £2.50.
Transport: riverboat to Kew Pier; train or tube to Kew Gardens.

With 38,000 species of plants and trees set amongst palm houses, follies and pagodas, an orangery and a 17th- century palace, Kew Gardens are among the most exotic in the world. Princess Augusta first planted the collection in the grounds of Kew Palace (a red-bricked Tudor mansion built

on the river in 1631, closed for renovation until 2001). George III opened the gardens to the public and commissioned William Chambers to build Kew's many follies, temples and summerhouses, the most famous of which is the 163ft-high Chinese Pagoda. In 1840 the gardens were given to the State, Decimus Burton's mammoth glasshouses were built, and plant laboratories were established which remain in use today. The Princess of Wales Conservatory, built in 1985 and one of Kew's most recent additions, contains a Titan Arum, one of the largest flowers in the world. The six-foot-high monster flowers every 2–4 years and bloomed for the first time in 1996, exuding a horrible stink that clung to the clothes of visitors and photographers.

KEW BRIDGE STEAM MUSEUM

Green Dragon Lane, Brentford, (020) 8568 4757.
Open: daily 11–5.
Admission: Sat–Sun £4, family ticket £10.50, concs £3, 5s–15s £2. Mon–Fri
£3, family ticket £7, concs £2, 5s–15s £1.
Transport: riverboat to Kew Pier; train to Kew Bridge.

In victorian times this 197ft standpipe tower pumped 22.6 million gallons of Thames water a day to homes in west London. Many Victorian waterworks had their own steam railways and examples of the locomotives are displayed on a short stretch of line – the prime ehibit is 'Cloister', a Hunslett engine, refurbished in the museum workshop. The museum is now the owner of five giant Cornish beam engines, two of which are demonstrated on weekends at 3pm. The engines

can be walked through while in steam, as can a section of Thames Water Ring Main documenting the history of water supply in London, and a sewer charting the history of sanitation from the 12th – 20th century.

KEW BRIDGE

Kew Bridge was built from Purbeck stone in 1903 and stands on the site of one of the first bridges across the Thames, built in 1749 by an enterprising ferryman. On the left bank is Strand-on-the-Green, a hamlet of fishermen's cottages with Dutch gables and steps leading up to the first floors to avoid flooding. Dylan Thomas, the poet, and Nancy Mitford, the novelist and arbiter of 'U' (upper-class) and 'non-U' behaviour, lived here in the 1930s.

FOOD AND DRINK

The City Barge

27 Strand-on-the-Green, (020) 8994 2148.
Food served: daily 12–10

This original Strand-on-the-Green pub has purpose-built watertight doors and dates from the 15th century.

CHISWICK BRIDGE

Chiswick Bridge marks the finishing line of the Oxford & Cambridge boat race and its central arch has the longest span of any bridge across the Thames. On its southeast side is the eight-storey Budweiser Brewery: the site is owned by the Archbishops of Canterbury and breweries have stood on it since 1427.

BARNES BRIDGE

The humpbacked railway bridge was built in 1849 out of prefabricated steel and includes a footway for pedestrians.

FOOD AND DRINK

Ye White Hart

The Terrace, Riverside, SW13, (020) 8876 5177.

Food served Mon–Sat 12.15–2, Sun 12.30–2.30.

This magnificent four-storey Victorian pub has expansive views up and down the river from three open balconies at the back, making it a choice venue for boat-race watchers.

HAMMERSMITH BRIDGE

Designed by Joseph Bazalgette (see 'Embankment' p44), in 1887, Hammersmith Bridge is a replica of an earlier suspension bridge of 1827 by Tierney Clark (who built the Szécheny Chain Bridge across the Danube, the first permanent connection between the royal seat of Buda and the modern city of Pest). In June 2000, dissident IRA members set off a small bomb beneath the bridge in the first terrorist attack on the mainland since devolution. The bridge was a symbolic target as it had been blown up by the IRA once before at the start of the Second World War in 1939.

FOOD AND DRINK

The Dove

19 Upper Mall, W6 (020) 8748 5405.

Food served daily 12–2.30 and 6.30–9.

The Dove is one of London's most celebrated river pubs, and its lovely conservatory and small verandah are wonderfully close-up to the river. The pub dates from the 17th century and in 1740 the Scottish poet James Thomson, recently retired to Richmond, wrote the words to 'Rule Britannia' in one of its upstairs rooms.

The Blue Anchor

13 Lower Mall, Hammersmith, (020) 8748 5774.

Food served: daily 12–4.

Situated on northwest side of Hammersmith Bridge and packed out in the summer.

HARRODS DEPOSITORY

In the early 1890s Harrods bought a soap factory nearby for use as a furniture depository. The purpose-built riverside distribution warehouse shown in this photograph was added in 1914 and features the same twin domes and salmon-pink terracotta façade as the Harrods store in Knightsbridge. In the late 1980s the whole site was developed into 'Harrods Village', a compound of 250 townhouses and luxury apartments which sold for up to £3 million for a riverside penthouse.

FULHAM FC

Fulham Football Club started as a church side (Fulham St Andrews) and moved to the grounds at Craven Cottage in 1896. For the next 100 years 'The Cottagers' floundered at the bottom of the league. Then in 1997 its fortunes turned dramatically around when Harrods' owner Mohamed Al Fayed bought the squad for £30 million and pledged to take it to the Premiership within five years. Fayed invested a further £40 million in the club and by 2000 Fulham had come top of the First Division.

PUTNEY BRIDGE

Designed by Joseph Bazalgette in 1886, Putney Bridge is the starting point for the Oxford & Cambridge Boat Race held annually in March. The course spans a 4.25-mile stretch from Putney to Mortlake and lasts about 17 minutes, with each boat vying to dominate a narrow strip of water where

23

the current flows fastest. Londoners crowd onto bridges and riverside pubs along the route and an estimated 500 million people watch it live on television.

On the south side of the bridge is the church of St Mary the Virgin where the Putney Debates were held in 1647. The debates were the first public discussion of democratic rights on record. During them the Levellers presented Cromwell with a radical programme for universal suffrage and religious toleration. Though some of his own officers supported the proposals, Cromwell rejected their demands and eventually suppressed the movement completely.

FOOD AND DRINK

The Putney Bridge

The Embankment, SW15, (020) 87801811.
Bar open: Mon–Thur noon–midnight, Fri–Sat 12–1am, Sun 12–10.30.
Restaurant open: Tue–Thur 12–2.30, 7–10.30, Fri–Sat 12–2.30, 6.30–11.
Set lunch: £18.50, set Sun lunch £24.50, set dinner £32.50.

The Putney Bridge also has a smart restaurant on the first floor serving excellent contemporary French cuisine.

Duke's Head

8 Lower Richmond Road, SW15, (020) 8940 6844.
Food served: daily 12–4.

On three floors overlooking the starting point for the boat race.

WANDSWORTH BRIDGE

Wandsworth Bridge is London's least glamorous but strongest bridge. Opened in 1937, the steel-girdered bridge withstands a daily onslaught of heavy goods vehicles hurtling in and out of London.

CHELSEA HARBOUR

This sleek riverside development incorporates a yachting harbour, hotel and 500 apartments, and was built in 1986 in less than a year. The Belvedere is a 20-storey apartment tower featuring an external glass lift and pyramid roof. A computerised golden ball at the top rises and falls to synchronise with the tides.

FOOD AND DRINK

The Ship

41 Jew's Row, SW18, (020) 8870 9667.
Open: Mon–Sat 11–11, Sun 12–10.30; food served: daily 12–10.30.
Main course: £7–11.
Transport: train to Wandsworth Town, 28 or 295 bus.

Packed out on summer evenings, this genial Victorian pub sits incongruously amidst industrial estates and a new luxury riverside development on the Wandsworth side of the river. Good inventive pub grub, including homemade sausage and mash.

LOTS ROAD POWER STATION & CHELSEA REACH HOUSEBOATS

Coal is no longer delivered here by barge, but the belching chimneys of the Lots Road Station still supply enough electricity for London Underground. The houseboats moored next to Battersea Bridge were originally used by livery companies for state occasions and then recycled as boat club HQs for the Oxford colleges. Nowadays the houseboats fetch up to £300,000 a piece and most have been converted for residential use, each one with its own postal address and electricity.

ST MARY'S BATTERSEA

London's only riverside church is known as Blake's Church, because it was here in 1782 that the poet and visionary William Blake married Catherine Boucher, the daughter of a local market gardener. The present building dates from 1777 and replaced an earlier church. A memorial inside commemorates Turner, who painted sunsets over the Thames from the vestry window.

CHEYNE WALK

The Georgian houses of Cheyne Walk were home to a succession of 19th-century creative luminaries including George Eliot, Henry James, Elizabeth Gaskell, Hilaire Belloc, Marc and Isambard Brunel, Philip Wilson Steer, Turner, Whistler, Swinburne, Meredith and Rossetti (who kept kangaroos, peacocks, owls and a wombat – supposedly the original of the dormouse in *Alice in Wonderland* – in his garden). The pastiche Tudor palace pictured overleaf was built in 1998 by a former deputy chairman of Lloyd's of London.

FOOD AND DRINK

Busabong Tree

112 Cheyne Walk, SW10, (020) 7352 7534.
Open: Mon–Sat 12–3, 6–11.15; Sun 12–3..
Main course: £8-16, set lunch from £9.95 for three courses.

Delicately cooked Thai food.

Ransome's Dock

35 Parkgate Road, SW11, (020) 7223 1611.
Open: Mon-Sat 11-11, Sun 12-3.30.
Main course: £10-20.

This bustling wharfside restaurant is based in a converted warehouse on the south side of Battersea Bridge.

BATTERSEA BRIDGE

The gold and green iron bridge with its distinctive Victorian gas lights was built in 1890 by Joseph Bazalgette. It replaced the simple 1772 timber bridge depicted in Whistler's *Nocturne in Blue and Silver* (now in Tate Britain).

CHELSEA OLD CHURCH
Cheyne Walk, SW3, (020) 7352 5627,
www.domini.org/chelsea-old-church
Open: Mon–Fri 12–4; Sun 8–1 and 2–7.
Admission: free.
Transport: riverboat to Cadogan Pier; tube to Sloane Square.

During the blitz, a German parachutist was found stumbling along the riverside after Chelsea Old Church was blasted by a bomb into a 'heap of timber and stone'. The 12th century church was completely restored after the war and contains a statue commemorating Thomas More, who was a regular at the church and built a chapel for his wife in the grounds. The statuette in the adjoining gardens of the church is by Derwent Woodra.

ALBERT BRIDGE

London's prettiest bridge was designed by Rowland Ordish in 1873. The 'sugar-spun' girders were not strong enough to support 20th-century heavy goods vehicles and, in the

1960s, the suspension bridge was scheduled for demolition. After much public protest the bridge was strengthened and shored up in the middle with two stone piers instead. Albert Bridge still bounces under the traffic, and notices on the toll kiosks at either end tell soldiers to 'break step' as they cross (a scenario envisaged in Tom Stoppard's radio play *Albert's Bridge*, in which the bridge collapses after 1,800 men march on to paint it).

FOOD AND DRINK

The King's Head & Eight Bells

50 Cheyne Walk, SW3, (020) 7352 1820.
Food served: Mon–Sat 12–10, Sun 12.30–4 and 7–10.

This quintessentially Chelsea pub was a favourite haunt of the writers and painters Whistler, Rossetti, George Eliot, Theodora Fitzgibbon, and Dylan and Caitlin Thomas.

CHELSEA PHYSIC GARDEN

66 Royal Hospital Road (Swan Walk entrance), SW3,
(020) 7352 5646,
www.cpgarden.demon.co.uk
Open: Apr–Oct, Wed 12–5 and Sun 2–6.
Admission: £4, concs and 5s-16s £2.
Transport: riverboat to Cadogan Pier; tube to Sloane Square.

The Physic Garden was founded in 1673 by the Society of Apothecaries for the 'manifestation of the glory, power and wisdom of God'. These days the physic garden still grows plants for medicinal purposes and regularly supplies samples to the pharmaceutical and fungal laboratories at Glaxo Wellcome and Imperial College. Several thousand varieties of herbs, fruits and vegetables are crammed into the remarkable 3.25 acre garden. The collection includes examples of woad (the blue dye used by the Romans), South Seas cotton seed (sent to America in 1732 to establish the first cotton fields in Georgia) and Britain's largest outdoor olive tree, which ripens in December and can produce 7lbs of olives a season.

BATTERSEA PARK &
THE LONDON PEACE PAGODA,
Albert Bridge Road, SW11, (020) 8871 7530.
Open: daily 8am-dusk.
Admission: free.
Transport: riverboat to Cadogan Pier; train to Battersea Park.

In 1842 Dickens described Battersea as 'a waste expanse' popular with duelists, bums and vagrants. In the next decade the marshes were filled in with a million cubic feet of earth from Victoria Docks and transformed into a genteel park. Nowadays Battersea Park includes an art gallery, deer enclosures and a children's zoo. The Peace Pagoda pictured here was given to the park by a Japanese Buddhist monastery and is one of 70 similar monuments around the world commemorating the bombing of Hiroshima.

CHELSEA ROYAL HOSPITAL

Royal Hospital Road, SW3,
(020) 7730 5282.
Open: Mon–Sat 10–12, 2–4 and Sun 2–4. Closed Sun in winter.
Admission: free.
Transport: riverboat to Cadogan Pier; tube to Sloane Square.

Charles II founded the Royal Hospital (designed by Christopher Wren and one of London's loveliest buildings) in 1682, supposedly after a one-legged veteran approached Nell Gwynn's coach and begged her for alms. Four hundred old boys still occupy the building and wear the distinctive 18th-century uniform of navy blue frock coats in winter and scarlet coats with three-cornered hats in the summer and on special occasions.

CHELSEA BRIDGE

Opened in 1937, this suspension bridge was built out of prefabricated sections and is much stronger than Albert Bridge. Chelsea Bridge comes into its own at night when it is draped, Sloane Ranger-style, in necklaces of pearly light bulbs.

THE CHELSEA BRIDGE BUNGEE JUMP

Open Fri 12–5 and Sat–Sun 11–6, closed Fri Oct–Mar, admission £50 or
£5 cage ride.
020 7720 9496

The ultimate in terror, this 300-foot plunge leaves bravest souls dangling above the Thames from the 'world's largest bungee tower'. For a mere £5, their less-brave companions can wacth them from a 'white knuckle' viewing platform.

CHELSEA TIDE-MILL

The tide-mill works alongside this Victorian water tower were installed by the Chelsea Waterworks Co., a private company formed in 1723. According to a petition to Parliament of 1827, the river water it extracted included 'the contents of the great common sewers, the drainings from dunghills, and laystalls, the refuse of hospitals, slaughter houses, colour, lead and soap works, drug mills and manufactories, and with all sorts of decomposed animal and vegetable substances, rendering the said water offensive and destructive to health...'

Londoners, who drink recycled Thames water to this day, can comfort themselves with the thought that in the last 50 years the Thames has become one of the cleanest urban rivers in the world. Salmon returned to the fishless river in 1973 and since then 115 other fish have been recorded including chub, pike, brown shrimp, flounder, mullet, whitebait and eel. In March 2000 tourists even identified a porpoise, leaping out of the water near the Houses of Parliament.

BATTERSEA POWER STATION

The inspiration for a Pink Floyd album cover, this coal-fired power station was designed in 1933 by Giles Gilbert Scott, the architect behind Bankside Power Station (now Tate Modern), Cambridge University Library and the classic British telephone box. It was put out of service in 1983 and left to go derelict while a succession of owners dithered over its future. In 2000, despite opposition from local community groups, the Hong Kong developers Parkview announced plans to turn the site into an entertainment, leisure, sport and retail park, complete with cinemas, restaurants, hotels, luxury flats, offices, theatres and a waterwall wedding pavilion by the Waterloo International station architect Nicholas Grimshaw. The redevelopment will include a 2,000 seater circus space for Cirque du Soleil, the award-winning Canadian circus troupe that was created in 1984 using entertainers from the streets of Quebec.

Scott's plans originally specified two square chimneys, and it was only after the station was doubled in size and two extra chimneys were added at either end in 1953 that the building began to resemble an enormous upside-down table with its legs in the air.

VAUXHALL BRIDGE

Vauxhall Bridge dates from 1905 and the large Art Nouveau superheroes on its piers symbolise science, agriculture, architecture, engineering and pottery.

In 1974 London's fruit, vegetable and flower market moved from Covent Garden to larger premises on the south side of Vauxhall Bridge at Nine Elms. The market stands nearby the site of Spring Gardens, the pleasure gardens which opened in 1661 and whose gothic ruins, waterfalls and arbours, accessible by boat, only remained a hugely popular London attraction until well into the middle of the 19th century.

LONDON SKY VIEW BALLOON
Spring Gardens, Vauxhall SE11,
020 7303 230350.
Open: spring–autumn, 10–dusk, weather permitting.
Admission: £12 per 15 minute ride.
Transport: tube to Vauxhall.

The helium-filled 'ballon captif' moored in Vauxhall Spring Gardens rises to a height of 400ft to give panoramic views of London. Ballooning – sometimes using hydrogen – was a craze in 18th century London: 'Balloons occupy senators, philosophers, ladies, everybody,' wrote Horace Walpole in 1785.

MI6
With its bottle-green walls, concrete spikes and cone-shaped trees, this perversely eye-catching fortress is the headquarters of MI6 or SIS and home to around 2,000 spies. Founded in 1909, MI6 is dedicated to gathering overseas intelligence (their sister organisation, MI5, is responsible for British intelligence and occupies less conspicuous premises across the river). In one of their jollier gestures, the Real IRA emulated action sequences from the James Bond film *The World is Not Enough* when they launched a Russian-built rocket missile at the building in September 2000, breaking an eighth floor window and charring curtains. The missile was a Mark 22 tank buster designed for blowing up tanks and capable of penetrating up to a metre of reinforced concrete. It was not powerful enough, however, to inflict

serious damage on this £230m building, designed by Terry Farrell in the early 1990s and incorporating a sophisticated mesh or 'Faraday Cage' which stops electromagnetic waves getting in or out of the premises. MI6 has had to resort to more old-fashioned technology (blinds) to prevent sightseers in boats videoing the 007s drinking gin and tonics in the riverside bar.

FOOD AND DRINK

The Morpeth Arms

58 Millbank, SW1, (020) 7834 6442.
Food served: daily 11.30–8.

Old-fashioned, very civilised Victorian pub, only a few steps away from Tate Britain.

TATE BRITAIN
Millbank, SW1,
(020) 7887 8000,
www.tate.org.uk
Open: daily 10–5.50.
Admission: free.
Transport: tube to Pimlico.

The world-famous collection of British art from 1500 to the present day was founded in 1897 by Henry Tate of Tate & Lyle. It has outstanding examples of Hogarth, Samuel Palmer, Constable, Blake and Stubbs, plus the unrivalled Clore Gallery collection comprising 300 oil paintings and 19,000 sketches by Turner. Every autumn the Tate hosts the media-friendly Turner Prize awarded to artists under 50. Throughout the year it also hosts temporary exhibitions of leading contemporary British artists.

Tate Britain stands on the site of the Millbank Gaol, built in 1812–21 and the largest penitentiary in Europe. The six- sided building incorporated elements of the panopticon design advocated by the prison reformer Jeremy Bentham, and included a central observation tower from which male and female inmates could be kept, *Big Brother*-style, under constant surveillance. A hexagonal outline of the gaol is still visible from the air today.

THE LOCKING PIECE

The Locking Piece, a large, orgiastic, fountain-lapped bronze sculpture by Henry Moore, at the foot of Vauxhall Bridge marks the point where convicts from Millbank Gaol were led down a flight of stairs for transportation to Australia.

MILLBANK TOWER

Built in 1963 Millbank Tower was once the tallest building in Europe. Decades later there was uproar in the press when the 387-ft hulk – a limp emulation of the classic New York glass-walled skyscraper – was given Grade II listing by

English Heritage. The tower gained further notoriety when the Labour Party made it their new headquarters in 1997, since when 'Millbank' has become synonymous with the New Labour media machine and its ministering spin doctors.

ALEMBIC HOUSE

Jeffrey Archer, London's disgraced mayoral candidate and literature's arch diabolo, lives in the enormous penthouse at the top of Alembic House overlooking the Houses of Parliament and surrounded by a £10m art collection which includes works by Lowry, Dufy, Sisley, Miro, Moore, Gerald Scarfe and Andy Warhol. Archer was forced to resign as Tory candidate for mayor in 1999 after a friend revealed he had lied on Archer's behalf during a trial in which Archer won £500,000 in damages after The *Daily Star* alleged he had a relationship with former prostitute Monica Coghlan. The *Daily Star* is currently trying to claim back its half a million, plus 15 years' interest.

LAMBETH BRIDGE & PALACE

Lambeth Bridge and its distinctive pineapple topped pylons was built in 1932. On its southeast side is Lambeth Palace, home to the Archbishops of Canterbury since 1190. Horseferry Road on the north side commemorates the lucrative ferry service for horses and coaches run by a succession of Archbishops of Canterbury until Westminster Bridge was built in 1750. On the south side is the Thames Fire Brigade's Floating Fire Station which was towed here from Wales in 1991 and incorporates sleeping quarters, offices, a lecture theatre, kitchens and a gym.

MUSEUM OF GARDEN HISTORY

St Mary-at-Lambeth Church, Lambeth Palace Road, SW1,
(020) 7261 1891,
www.cix.co.uk.~museumgh
Open: Feb, Mon–Fri 11-2; Mar–Dec, Mon–Fri 10.30–4, Sun 10.30–5.
Admission: free.
Transport: riverboat to Westminster Millennium Pier.

This small museum in the grounds of St Mary's is based around the work of the 17th century collector and royal gardener John Tradescant, who brought fritillaries and mulberry trees to England from Europe, and whose 'Ark' of weird and wonderful curiosities evolved eventually into the Ashmolean Museum in Oxford. The gardens contain Tradescant's tomb and the grave of Captain Bligh, who was cast adrift from the HMS *Bounty* after his crew mutinied near the South Sea island of Tahiti. Bligh and the 18 men who stayed loyal to him managed to survive a 3,600-mile journey in an open boat, reaching Timor two months later in June 1789.

ST THOMAS' HOSPITAL

St Thomas' moved here from Southwark in 1871. Most of the original hospital has been replaced by modern buildings, but Florence Nightingale's training school for nurses remains and qualified nurses or 'Nightingales' still wear the same caps, worn back to front, as their mentor.

THE HOUSES OF PARLIAMENT

Parliament Square, SW1,
Commons info (020) 7219 4272,
Lords info (020) 7219 3107,
www.parliament.uk
Open: House of Commons Visitors' Gallery: Mon–Tues from 2.30, Wed
9.30–2, Thur 11.30–7.30, Fri 9.30–3. House of Lords Visitors' Gallery:
Mon–Wed from 2.30, Thur from 3, Fri from 11.
Admission: free.
Transport: riverboat to Westminster Millennium Pier; tube to
Westminster.

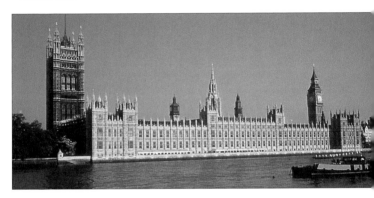

The present Houses of Parliament replaced the Royal Palace of Westminster, built originally for King Canute, then rebuilt and enlarged by Edward the Confessor and William the Conqueror. On 16 October 1834 a fire in furnaces beneath the House of Lords raged out of control and Londoners flocked to the scene in boats and cheered as the flames leapt higher into the skies and the palace all but burnt to the ground, a scene graphically recreated in an 1835 painting by Turner. A competition for a 'Gothic or Elizabethan style' replacement building was won by Charles Barry who worked tirelessly on the project for 25 years with the help of Augustus Pugin, the 24-year-old genius behind the dazzling Gothic ornamentation. Today a flag flying on top of the Victoria Tower to the west indicates that Parliament is sitting.

BIG BEN

St Stephen's Tower got its nickname from Sir Benjamin Hall, the unusually tall Commissioner of Works who was blamed for the many mishaps which delayed completion of the building until 1859. Big Ben has seldom stopped by accident, although its hands have been known to seize up under the weight of snow and flocks of starlings. The clock's pendulum is 13ft long and pennies regulate its swings to two-fifths of a second. The chimes are based on an aria from Handel's Messiah, and the words accompanying the ding-dong-ding-dong are:

All through this hour
Lord be my guide
And by Thy Power
No foot shall slide [BONG].

In 1997, as works on the Westminster extension to the Jubilee line got underway, Big Ben began to tilt. A Leaning Tower of Pisa expert was called in and 300 tonnes of grout were injected into its foundations. Now, although it has been stabilised, Big Ben leans an inch and a half to one side.

PORTCULLIS HOUSE

Designed by Michael Hopkins in 1999, Portcullis House was built to house offices for 200 MPs at a cost of £250 million (over £1 million per MP). Fig trees for the restaurant cost £200,000 alone, and the interior, with its thick-pile carpets and leather armchairs equipped with snooze buttons, is as lavish as the bronze clad and sandstone neo-Gothic exterior.

Costs aside, Portcullis House has a certain presence and it fits, strangely well, and with the peculiar grace of heavyweight boxer, into this very conspicuous site next to Big Ben and the Houses of Parliament.

WESTMINSTER BRIDGE & THE SOUTH BANK LION

For 700 years, until the opening of Westminster Bridge in 1750, London Bridge was the city's only river crossing. Westminster Bridge was a toll-free bridge and it was not long before it destroyed the livings of some 40,000 watermen who plied for hire up and down the Thames. While Wordsworth dedicated a poem to it (*Upon Westminster Bridge*), James Boswell's consecration was more literal: 'I picked up a strong jolly young damsel,' the Scottish diarist wrote, 'and taking her under the arm I conducted her to Westminster Bridge, and then in armour complete [donning a condom] did I engage up in this noble edifice. The whim of doing it there with the Thames rolling below us amused me much.'

Keep an eye out for the 'South Bank Lion', guarding Westminster Bridge from a plinth on its southwest corner. The handsome beast was sculpted for the Lion Brewery, which stood on the South Bank and was heavily bombed in the Blitz. The lion is made from Coade Stone, an extremely hard-wearing pollution-resistant artificial stone made of sand, flint, glass and clay which was invented in 1769 and manufactured at a factory near County Hall.

THE EMBANKMENTS

During the heatwave of 30 June 1858 the House of Commons adjourned after panic broke out over the 'great stink' coming off the Thames. To get rid of the smell lime was piled into the river and the House of Commons windows were hung with sheets soaked in chloride disinfectant. A statue near Charing Cross Bridge commemorates Sir Joseph Bazalgette, the man who tackled the problem of the open sewers which were causing cholera outbreaks all over London. Bazalgette's solution was to bury the sewers underground and divert their flow away from the centre (where most drinking water was still drawn) and out into the Thames estuary. The scheme, completed in 1875 at a cost of £6.5 million, created the Victoria and Chelsea Embankments, a 3.5 mile stretch of promenades and gardens furnished with decorative cast-iron dolphin lamps and griffin benches.

COUNTY HALL

Westminster's palace of bureaucracy was built in 1909–22 to house the mandarins of the London County Council (LCC) and its successor the Greater London Council (GLC). In 1986 Mrs Thatcher abolished the GLC and its outspoken leader Ken Livingstone, whose 'loony left' policies had been a constant irritation. In May 2000 Livingstone stood as an independent and, riding on a wave of populist support, trounced both the Labour and Conservative official candidates to become the first elected Mayor of London.

After the abolition of the GLC, County Hall was sold to a Japanese consortium for £60 million. An odd assortment of attractions now fills a mostly underexploited building, the most worthwhile of which are the London Aquarium and the Dalí Universe. A more expensive proposition is Namco Station, (open daily 10-midnight, www.namco.co.uk), a two floor Playstation and video game complex with fruit machines, DJs on weekends and the fastest bumper cars in Europe.

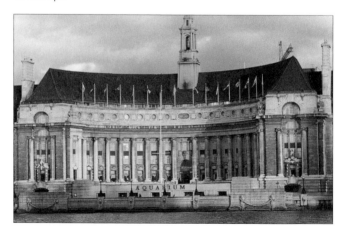

THE LONDON AQUARIUM

County Hall, Riverside Building, Westminster Bridge Road, SE1,
(020) 7967 8000,
www.londonaquarium.co.uk
Open: daily 10–6, last entry 5.
Admission: £8.50, concs £6.40, 3s-14s £5, free to wheelchair users and
under 5s.
Transport: riverboat to Westminster Millennium Pier; tube to
Westminster or train/tube to Waterloo.

Walking down the gently sloping concrete ramp into the dark and glimmering depths of the London Aquarium is disconcertingly like a return to the womb. Now, deep down in the basement of County Hall, where GLC councillors once munched their sandwiches and Golden Wonder crisps, is a more mysterious world, populated by giant groupers, piranhas, carpet sharks, stingrays, long horned cowfish, jellyfish, sea horses and octopus. The centrepiece is a three-storey cylindrical tank containing shoals of shark and seabass, fed each day on squid and mackerel by teams of dauntless divers. Elsewhere the aquarium takes in freshwater, ocean, coral reef, mangrove swamp and rain-forest habitats, some with trickling sound effects and phony Easter Island ruins. For youngsters there are touch pools where star fish, ray and crabs can be picked up and stroked.

DALÍ UNIVERSE

County Hall, Riverside Building, Westminster Bridge Road, SE1
(020) 7620 2420, www.daliuniverse.com
Open: daily 10–5.30.
Admission: £8.50, 5s-16s £5, under 5s free, family ticket £20, concs £6.

Most of the sculptures, graphics, jewellery, furniture, drawings and watercolours at this enjoyable exhibition hale from late on in Dalí's career, when fellow Surrealists accused

'Aveda Dollars' of betraying the movement and shamelessly commercialising art for his own financial gain. While most of the exhibits are not vintage Dalí, their entertainment quotient is reliably high. Star exhibits include an 'all in the best possible taste' Mae West lips sofa, lurid drawings from the *Secret Life* autobiography, and the giant eye and eyelashes painted for the dream sequence in Hitchcock's *Spellbound*.

FOOD AND DRINK

The Four Regions

County Hall, SE1, (020) 7928 0988..
Open: daily 12–3, 6–11.30.
Main course: £8–12.

Lovely views of the Houses of Parliament and British Airways London Eye make up for the good but unamazing food at this Chinese restaurant.

RS Hispaniola

Victoria Embankment, WC2, (020) 7839 3011.
Open: daily 12–2.30, and Mon–Sat 6.30–11.
Main course: £20.

International fare, plus jazz piano on weekends.

THE BRITISH AIRWAYS LONDON EYE

Jubilee Gardens, near County Hall, SE1
advance booking: (0870) 500 0600
www.ba-londoneye.com
Open: Apr–Oct, daily 9–dusk; Nov–Mar, daily 10–6.
Admission: £7.45, concs £5.95, 5s-15s £4.95.
Transport: riverboat to Westminster Millennium Pier; tube to Westminster or train/tube to Waterloo.

The giant bicycle wheel is a sight to gladden the hearts of Londoners and a brilliantly conceived addition to the London skyline. It's also the world's highest observation wheel: on clear days views from the top extend for up to 25 miles, as far as Windsor to the west and Gravesend to the east. Designed by David Marks and Julia Barfield, the wheel moves at such a dignified pace that at first glance it seems stationary. Each one of the 32 capsules takes exactly half an hour to complete a 450-ft arc into the sky. Come at sunset for the most spectacular views or at night for the most romantic.

CLEOPATRA'S NEEDLE

This 3,500 year old obelisk (a twin to the Cleopatra's Needle in Manhattan) was given to Britain by the Viceroy of Egypt in 1819. The 186-ton monolith was carved by the Pharaohs in 1500 BC and stood in Alexandria during Cleopatra's lifetime.

CHARING CROSS STATION & NEW HUNGERFORD BRIDGES

Looking like a Viking's helmet, this imposing new office complex and railway shed was built on top of Charing Cross Station in 1990. The word 'Charing' comes from the Anglo-Saxon word *cerr*, meaning a bend in the river, and the 'cross' in Charing Cross refers to the last of the 12 crosses put up by Edward I to mark the route taken by Eleanor of Castile's funeral cortège. In 2001, two new footbridges linking the South Bank to the West End will be built alongside Brunel's original Hungerford Railway Bridge.

THE SOUTH BANK CENTRE

South Bank, Belvedere Road, SE1,
Box office: (020) 7960 4242,
recorded info: (020) 7921 0682, www.sbc.org.uk
Transport: riverboat to Festival Pier; tube or train to Waterloo.

The Festival Hall was built for the Festival of Britain in 1951, but was soon joined by four other South Bank mainstays: the Hayward Gallery (one of London's most vibrant modern art venues), the Queen Elizabeth Hall, the Purcell Room and the National Theatre. There are free lunchtime concerts in the Festival Hall foyer every day, 12.30–2pm.

THE HAYWARD GALLERY NEON TOWER

Designed by Philip Vaughan and Roger Dainton for a Kinetics exhibition at the Hayward in 1970, the tower's neon strips change colour according to changes in wind speed and direction.

FOOD AND DRINK

The People's Palace

Level 3, Festival Hall.
(020) 7928 9999.
Open: daily 12–3, 5.30–11.
Main course: £12–17.

Laidback restaurant on Level 3 of the Festival Hall with stupendous river views.

The Archduke

Concert Hall Appraoch, South Bank SE1.
(020) 7428 9370
Open: Mon–Sat 12–2.15, 5.30–11, Sat 5.30–11
Main course: £7–12.

Wine bar under railway arches featuring a speciality sausage menu.

BFI LONDON IMAX CINEMA

Waterloo Building, South Bank, SE1,
(020) 7902 1234,
www.bfi.org.uk
Open: up to seven screenings daily, Mon–Fri 11–8.45, Sat–Sun 11–10pm.
Admission: £6.75, concs £5.75, 5s-16s £4.75, under 5s free.
Transport: riverboat to Festival Pier; train or tube to Waterloo.

Rising phoenix-like from a depressing concrete roundabout outside Waterloo Station, this big glass drum is the biggest and most technically advanced IMAX in Europe. The 500-seat theatre sits on hydraulic springs to soften the roar of the cars, trains and tubes around it and inside up to 49 IMAX films a week are projected on a screen the size of five double decker buses.

IMAX films in 2 & 3D were developed originally in the 1970s using cameras as big as suitcases and 350mm film.

One day, probably, all films will be produced in IMAX format: Steven Spielberg is said to be exploring its potential the BBC has recently invested £8m in an IMAX documentary on the human body. Though 2001 will see the premiere of *Cyberworld*, a 3D cartoon feature starring Antz and The Simpsons, you should also brace yourself for subject matter ranging from the worthy and stupendous (nature documentaries such as *Into the Deep*, exploring the underwater coast of California) to the wondrous and bizarre (Paul Cox's *Four Million Houseguests*, a vertiginous journey via an illuminator super-microscope into the mysterious world of giant-size carpets, rotting fruit and Velcro).

WATERLOO BRIDGE & THE FLOATING THAMES POLICE STATION

With its perennially constipated traffic and insect-like swarms of commuters, this is the bridge that inspired the Kinks' 1967 hit, 'Waterloo Sunset' ('As long as I gaze on Waterloo Sunset, I am in paradise'). The stark, utilitarian bridge was designed in 1939 by Giles Gilbert Scott, the architect behind Battersea and Bankside Power Stations. It replaced a York stone toll-bridge of 1817.

On the north side is the floating Thames Police Station, the headquarters of the marine police force established by Jeremy Bentham in 1798. Crime on the river is still rife and Thames Division recover an average of £6m in drugs, boats and marine equipment every year, as well as between 80 and 100 bodies, 80 per cent of which are suicides.

SOMERSET HOUSE: THE GILBERT COLLECTION, HERMITAGE ROOMS & COURTAULD GALLERY

Somerset House, Strand, WC2,
(020) 7845 4600,
www.somerset-house.org.uk
Open: Mon–Sat 10–6, Sun 12–6.
Admission: joint adm £7, concs £5.
Transport: riverboat to Embankment or Savoy Pier; tube to Charing Cross.

William Chambers' Somerset House was tailor-made in 1776 to house a range of government offices and learned societies, and replaced a grand Renaissance palace built on the site in 1547 by Lord Protector Somerset. In 1999 the entire building got a £48 million revamp and two new museums were added along with shops, restaurants and 55 water jet fountains in the newly opened Courtyard. The South Building now contains the Gilbert Collection, a display of European jewellery, mosaics and portrait miniatures, and The Hermitage Collection, a sumptuous recreation of five suites from the Hermitage in St Petersburg showcasing objects, paintings and other treasures from the museum. Somerset House remains home to the Inland Revenue and, rather more pleasantly, to the Courtauld Institute's outstanding collection of Impressionist and Post-Impressionist paintings. As well as key works such as Van Gogh's *Bandaged Ear*, Manet's *Bar at the Folies Bergère* and Cézanne's *Montagne Sainte-Victoire*, the Courtauld has many important Old Masters (works by Cranach, Tiepolo and Gainsborough) and a fine contemporary collection with work by the well known British abstractionist David Taborn.

In winter, the courtyard houses an open-air ice skating rink which organisers hope will become as much a part of London's Christams as the Rockerfeller Center's rink is New York.

LONDON WEEKEND TELEVISION

Free tickets available:
(020) 7261 3261, but call at least a month in advance.

The studios in this tower are used for recording such timeless productions as *Blind Date, Barrymore, Don't Try This At Home* and *So Graham Norton*.

FOOD AND DRINK

The Admiralty

Somerset House, WC2,
(020) 7845 4646.

Bar open: daily 11–11pm. Restaurant open: Mon–Sat 12–2.45, 6–10.45, Sun 12–2.45. Main course: £7–19.

Gourmet Pizza Co

1 Gabriel's Wharf, 56 Upper Ground, SE1.
(020) 7928 3188.
Open: daily 12–3.15, 5.30–11.
Main course: £5–10.

The humble pizza conquers the world at this globe-trotting restaurant, with toppings that assimilate every conceivable cuisine, from South American to Southeast Asian.

THE NATIONAL THEATRE
For 1 hour backstage tours Mon–Sat at 10.15 and 12.30 or 12.15
020 7452 3400,
www.nt-online.org

If proof was ever needed that concrete does not suit the English climate, Denys Lasdun's National Theatre building is it. Even so, the three world-famous stages inside make it one of London's most vibrant theatre venues. A network of foyers, restaurants, espresso bars and drama bookshops connects to Theatre Square, a new riverside plaza where a variety of free outdoor performance events are held.

GABRIEL'S WHARF
Gabriel's Wharf is a great place to stop for lunch or a snack: as well as three laidback restaurants, crêperies and bars there are 14 craft stalls selling affordable hand-produced ceramics, textiles, greetings cards, clothing and jewellery.

OXO TOWER WHARF
020 7401 2255,
www.oxotower.co.uk

Originally a power station, Oxo Tower wharf was built at the turn of the 20th century to supply electricity to the Post Office. In the 1920s it was taken over by Oxo, who used it as a cold store for meat and for processing the never-ending hard-boiled eggs inserted into pork pies to this day. Oxo added the magnificent Art Deco tower in 1930 and, when the architect Albert Moore was refused permission to spell out the brand name in electric lights, he neatly side-stepped 1930s' advertising restrictions by working the letters 'OXO' into the brickwork of the three vertically stacked windows at the top.

In the 1970s Oxo left the warehouse and developers moved in hoping to demolish the tower and replace it with Europe's largest skyscraper hotel and a million square feet of office space including a 20-storey office block by Richard Rogers. English Heritage refused to give the warehouse listed status but' in 1984, after a long drawn out battle with residents and local community groups, the wharf was rescued and sold to the non-profit making Coin Street

Community Builders for mixed-use redevelopment.

Now, after a magnificent £20 million refurbishment, the Oxo Tower has become a model of mixed-used inner city regeneration, combining social housing in the form of affordable co-op flats for 200 people with restaurants, cafes and bars and, uniquely, retail design studios. The ground floor has an information centre, with maps and a directory of the building, plus an art gallery (the.gallery@oxo) and an innovative exhibition space, the Museum Of ... On the first and second floors some of the best and latest in British contemporary design and couture is showcased at the prestigious Oxo Tower Designer Workshops (look out in particular for the award-winning enamelled jewellery in Studio Fusion). At the top of the tower alongside the trendy Oxo Tower Restaurant & Brasserie is a free public viewing gallery with glitzy views across the London skyline.

FOOD AND DRINK

Oxo Tower Bar, Restaurant and Brasserie

Oxo Tower Wharf, Barge House Street, SE1
(020) 7803 3888.
Bar open: Mon–Sat 11–11, Sun 12–10.30. Brasserie open: daily 12–3.30, Mon–Sat 5.30–11.30, Sun 6–10.30. Restaurant open: Mon–Sat 12-3, 6–11.30, Sun 12–3.30, 6–10.
Main course: £15–23.50, set lunch £20 (brasserie) £27 (restaurant).

Needless to say, Oxo cubes are held in utter contempt at this Harvey Nichols eaterie where east and western cuisines fuse with incredible views of the London skyline. The noisy diners and trendified food make the bar (facing south) a more restful alternative.

THE MUSEUM OF...

The Bargehouse, Oxo Tower Wharf, Bargehouse Street, SE1,
(020) 7928 1255
www.themuseumof.org
Open: Tues–Sun 11–6, last entry 5.30.
Admission: free.
Transport: riverboat to Blackfriars Millennium Pier, train or tube to Waterloo or Blackfriars.

This quirky and innovative museum is a venue for experimental temporary exhibitions challenging the way we think about museums. Themes so far have ranged from 'the unknown' (an exhibition of mysterious objects), to 'emotions' and 'me'. By 2002 the museum will host a permanent River Thames Discovery Centre devoted to the the history of the Thames.

COIN STREET FESTIVAL

From May to September this part of the South Bank hosts the Coin Street Festival, one of London's most vibrant arts festivals. As well as fiestas, circuses and fireworks displays, there are hundreds of free outdoor dance and music performances featuring a dazzling spectrum of Asian Underground, Gypsy, Cuban, Brazilian, Hybrid, Bluegrass and contemporary African sounds.

THE OLD BARGEHOUSE STAIRS & THAMES LIDO

The Bargehouse Stairs, a steep flight of steps leading down to the river, was a kind of 18th century taxi rank, used by London's ferrymen for setting down and picking up their fares. Londoners were notoriously fond of hurling insults at fellow passengers, and Samuel Johnson was said to be especially proud of his own 'Sir, your wife, under pretence of keeping a bawdy house, is a receiver of stolen goods'.

Archeologists digging along this stretch of river have found sunken wherries and lighters, remnants of a period when traffic on the Thames was busier than on roads. Other choice finds from what functioned as a communal rubbish dump for many centuries have included 17th-century Delftware, clay pipes, medieval pots, 15th-century wine bottles, Roman pots and jewellery, cattle bones and pigs' teeth.

Plans are afoot to moor a floating swimming pool, the new Thames Lido, near Bernie Spain Gardens at the end of a 40-metre jetty. Designed by Lifschutz Davidson, the futuristic egg-shaped steel swimming pool will rise and fall with the tides, giving local and professional swimmers an incredible 360° view of the city around them.

THE TEMPLE

The large stone archway here on the Embankment was designed by Sir Joseph Bazalgette to mark Temple Stairs, a stone staircase leading down to the river where Londoners could catch boats. Behind the stairs is The Temple, home from about 1160 to the Knights Templar, a military order dedicated to winning back the Holy Land from Muslim control. During the Crusades the monks turned their hands moneylending, so successfully that the order was suppressed by the Pope. In 1609 James I gave the property to the Bar for use as chambers, and barristers inhabit The Temple to this day.

FOOD AND DRINK

El Barco Latino

Temple Pier, Victoria Embankment, WC2.
(020) 7379 5496.
Open: daily 12pm-3am.
Admission: £6 after 9pm for non-diners (includes free drink).

Spanish and Colombian food, with Latin dancing on Fri and Sat evenings.

Doggett's Coat and Badge

1 Blackfriars Bridge, SE1.
(020) 7633 9081.
Food served: daily 12-3.

On the south side of Blackfriars Bridge, Doggett's Coat and Badge Pub dates from 1976 but commemorates a boat-race for apprentice watermen inaugurated by Irish actor Thomas Doggett in 1715. The race, run by teams of six from here to Cadogan Pier in Chelsea, is still held annually in the summer.

BLACKFRIARS BRIDGE

Blackfriars' 15 minutes of infamy came on 15 June 1992, when the Italian banker Roberto Calvi was found hanging from the its latticed girders. Calvi's bank collapsed soon after and, four years later, his financial adviser died of cyanide poisoning. Blackfriars is the widest bridge along the Thames, and one of the handsomest (though critics made fun of its red granite pulpits when it was put up in the 1860s). The name comes from an order of Dominican Black Friars established on the north side of the river in the 1220s (a company of Carmelite White Friars lived nearby). The area degenerated into one of London's rankest, partly because butchers from Smithfield market used to dump their offal in the Fleet, a small tributary which still flows into the Thames via a conduit near Blackfriars.

FOOD AND DRINK

The Blackfriar

(north side of Blackfriars Bridge), 174 Queen Victoria Street, EC4.
(020) 7236 5650.
Food served: Mon–Sat 12–2.30, Mon–Fri 5.30–9.

With the words 'WISDOM IS RARE' inscribed above the entrance, this pub features one of London's most exquisite art nouveau interiors, sculpted by Henry Poole in the early 1900s.

Laughing Gravy

(south side of Blackfriars Bridge) 154 Blackfriars Road, SE1.
(020) 7721 7055.
Open: Mon–Fri 11–11, Sat 6–11.
Main course: £12–15.

Smart modern European food, but there is a snack menu too.

LONDON, CHATHAM & DOVER RAILWAY CREST

The fat red columns in this photograph are piers from a railway bridge put up in the 1860s but dismantled 20 years later. The brightly-painted London, Chatham & Dover Railway crest on the south side of the river comes from the railway bridge and was one of its original abutments.

TATE MODERN

25 Sumner Street, SE1,
(020) 7401 5120,
car park for wheelchair users (020) 7887 8008,
www.tate.org.uk
Open: Mon–Thur & Sun 10–6, Fri–Sat 10–10.
Admission: free.
Transport: riverboat to Blackfriars Millennium Pier; tube to Southwark.

This immense and inspiring collection of international modern art opened in May 2000 and almost immediately established itself as a powerhouse of art to rival the Pompidou in Paris, MoMA in New York and the Guggenheim in Bilbao.

Designed in 1947 by Giles Gilbert Scott, Bankside Power Station was situated amidst the industrial slums of Southwark but provided electricity for the rookeries of offices on the other side of the river in the City. Now the dour industrial exterior (looking like a brooding backdrop from Fritz Lang's film *Metropolis*) contrasts stunningly with the crisp lines, high ceilings and swathes of natural light which Swiss architects Herzog & de Meuron cut into the interior. Though most of the station had to be gutted before the conversion began, the architects retained the existing turbine hall, scooped it out to basement level and added a huge ramped entrance as broad as a street. The power station was then flooded with light via a glass canopy which spans the entire building, adding two floors to its height and giving visitors spectacular views across the river to St Paul's and the City.

One hundred thousand square feet of galleries inside house a titanic collection arranged, refreshingly, along thematic rather than chronological lines. The many groundbreaking works on show include Jean Tinguely's *Memorial to the Sacred Wind*, a scrapyard 'happening machine' (which the gallery starts up daily every hour on the hour), Arshile Gorky's sexually charged masterpiece *Waterfall*, a lucent site specific wall drawing by Sol Lewitt, and Bill Viola's brain-mushing video installation, the *Nantes Triptych* which pitches images of a young woman giving birth and a man plunging into water against a video of an old woman (Viola's own mother) dying. The gallery received its own iconoclastic baptism by urine when, shortly after it opened, Yuan Cai and J. J. Xi relieved themselves on Duchamp's *Fountain*, a replica of the urinal exhibited at the New York Armoury Show in 1917. A French artist, Pierre Pinoncelli, had staged an identical assault on a Pompidou-owned Duchamp urinal in 1993, although in his case he was fined £30,000.

FOOD AND DRINK

Café Level Seven at Tate Modern

7th floor, Tate Modern, Sumner Street, SE1.
(020) 7401 5020..
Open: daily 10.15–3, and Fri–Sat 6.30–9.30.
Main course: £5.50–16.

From delicatessen-quality sandwiches to fish 'n chips and seared calves' liver.

THE MILLENNIUM BRIDGE

The bridge that wobbled had a notoriously shaky start in life when 200,000 people – five times more than expected – turned out to cross it on its opening weekend in June 2000. As crowds walked along in celebratory step, the £18.2 million bridge began to sway as much as eight inches to the side. Two days later the bridge was closed, and will remain so until engineers have figured out a way to fix some flexible shock absorbers to its underside. The elegant bridge – designed by the British sculptor Anthony Caro with the architect Norman Foster and engineers Ove Arup – spans 320 metres, linking the Tate Modern to St Paul's and restoring breathtaking vistas of the Thames to both sides of the river.

FOOD AND DRINK

The Bridge

1 Paul's Walk, off High Timber Street, EC4.
(020) 7236 0000.
Open: Mon–Fri 11–11pm, Sat–Sun 11–6.
Main course: £11-13.

On the St Paul's side of the Millennium Bridge, with outdoor terraces and eastern food including all-day dim sum.

ST PAUL'S CATHEDRAL

St Paul's Churchyard, SE1.
(020) 7236 4128.
www.stpaulslondon.anglican.org
Open: Mon–Sat 8.30–4, galleries, crypt and ambulatory 10-4.
Admission: £5, concs £4, 6s-16s £2.50.
Transport: riverboat to Blackfriars Millennium Pier, tube to St Paul's.

St Paul's was one of 52 London churches rebuilt by Christopher Wren after the Great Fire of 1666. The previous church caught light on 3 September 1666, generating such heat that the corpse of a 250-year-old Bishop of London blasted out of its grave and landed in the churchyard: 'The stones of St Paul's flew like grenados,' John Evelyn wrote in his diary, 'the melting lead running down the streets in a stream, and the very pavements glowing with fiery rednesses, so as no man nor horse was able to tread on them.' Four churches, the first dating from Anglo-Saxon times, had stood on the site and, from the laying of the first stone in 1675, the fifth St Paul's took 35 years to complete. Wren's tomb, with its inscription *'Si monumentum requiris, circumspice'* ('If you seek his monument, look around you'), is in the south choir aisle.

SHAKESPEARE'S GLOBE

New Globe Walk, Bankside, SE1.
(020) 7902 1500,.
www.shakespeares-globe.org
Exhibition open: May-Sept, daily 9-12.30; Oct-Apr, daily 10-5.
Exhibition admission: £7, concs £6, 5s-15s £5, family ticket £23 (includes guided tour Oct-Apr only).
Transport: tube to Southwark, train or tube to London Bridge.

In Shakespeare's day until the 18th century Bankside was a honeypot of sin, bursting with inns, brothels and bull-baiting rings where tethered bulls were killed by mastiff dogs. The barbaric shows were relished by citizens of every class, from the lowliest to Elizabeth I (it was 'good sport', Pepys wrote, but 'a very rude and nasty pleasure').

The new Globe Theatre stands on the site of one of Bankside's biggest bull-baiting arenas and only a few hundred feet away from the original Wooden O where **Romeo and Juliet, King Lear** and *Hamlet* were first performed. With its pristine thatch and timber-frame roof, the open-air playhouse takes authenticity to its fastidious extreme: costumes are dyed in urine, productions experiment with gender crossing and, short of throwing rotten eggs, audiences are encouraged to participate. Four plays are staged in repertory from May to September (as well as covered bench seating there is an open-air standing area where 'groundlings' prepared to brave the elements can get in for as little as £5). A permanent exhibition focuses on every aspect of Elizabethan drama, and there are guided tours backstage when the theatre is not performing.

SOUTHWARK BRIDGE & CANNON STREET STATION

With its steel arches, granite piers and understated grace, Southwark Bridge opened in 1921. Next to Southwark Bridge, a railway bridge leads to the yellow bricked Italianate spires of Cannon Street Station.

FOOD AND DRINK

Shakespeare's Globe

New Globe Walk, SE1.
(020) 7928 9444.
Open: daily 12–2.30, 6–10.
Main course: £12–17.

Excellent modern European-style cuisine.

The Anchor (south side of Southwark Bridge)

34 Park Street, SE1.
(020) 7407 1577.
Food served: daily 12–7.

This labyrinthine Victorian pub has five bars and two dining rooms. Two brothels, The Castle on the Hoop and The Gonne, originally stood on the site and were run by the Bishops of Winchester, whose cruelly treated prostitutes were nicknamed 'Winchester's Geese'. The pub was built the 15th century: Pepys and Samuel Johnson were regulars, and it was here, as Mark Turner points out in his excellent guide to the *Pubs of the River Thames*, that Johnson informed a lady who told him that he smelt, "You are mistaken madam. You smell, I stink."

VINOPOLIS, CITY OF WINE

1 Bank End, SE1.
(0870) 444 477.
www.vinopolis.co.uk.
Open: daily 10–5.
Admission: £11.50, OAPs £10.50, 5s-18s £4.50, £1 discount if booked in advance.
Transport: riverboat to London Bridge City Pier; train or tube to London Bridge.

Based in 2.5 acres of railway arches near London Bridge, Vinopolis is the wino's fantasy come true. The brainchild of wine merchant Duncan Arbuckle, the viticultural themepark includes tasting halls, wine bars, modern art works and a wine emporium selling every imaginable accoutrement including 43 different types of corkscrew. The centrepiece is a jolly if not totally belief-suspending virtual wine odyssey where you can tour Tuscany on a Vespa or test your sense of smell while listening to commentaries by Jancis Robinson, Oz Clark, Hugh Johnson *et al*. All visitors get to sample up to five different wines from a list of 200 (the total equivalent of a standard 12.5cl wine glass, so you shouldn't feel unduly pressured to spit it out).

FOOD AND DRINK

Vinopolis Wine Wharf

Stoney Street, SE1.
(020) 7940 8335..
Open: Mon–Fri 11–11pm, Sat–Sun 11–9; bar snacks served Mon–Fri 12–10pm, Sat–Sun 12–6.
Bar food: £2.50–7.50.

With an exhaustive wine list and classy *tapas*-style bar food.

Cantina Vinopolis

1 Bank End, SE1.
(020) 7940 8333.
Open: Mon–Fri 10–10pm, Sat–Sun 11–9 (wine bar); Mon–Sat 12–2.45, 6–10.15, Sun 12–3.45 (brasserie).
Main course: £11.50–14.

Four hundred wines and good value French/Italian modern cooking.

Petit Robert

3 Park Street, SE1.
(020) 7357 7003.
Open: Mon–Sat 6–10
Main course: £12–18

Delightful small bistro offering inventive French cooking.

THE GOLDEN HINDE

St Mary Overie Dock, Cathedral Street, SE1.
(020) 7403 0123.
www.goldenhinde.co.uk
Open: daily 10–6 (phone to check).
Admission: £2.50, concs £2, 4s-13s £1.75; tea and coffee available.
Transport: riverboat to London Bridge City Pier; train or tube to London Bridge.

This galleon is a meticulously detailed replica of the *Golden Hinde* which Francis Drake used to circumnavigate the world in 1580. Drake came back to England with £600,000 of South Seas booty (the equivalent of £60 million today), having claimed 'Nova Albion' or California along the way, or so the story goes. The Devon-built reconstruction here in St Mary Overie has sailed 100,000 miles across the world, many more than the original *Golden Hinde*. A crew dressed in 16th-century costume and consisting of master. mate, cook and 12 deckhands lives permanently aboard.

FOOD AND DRINK

Old Thameside Inn

Pickfords Wharf, Clink Street, SE1.
(020) 7403 4243.
Food served: Mon–Fri 12–2.30, Sat–Sun 12–4

This well run pub is based in a converted spice warehouse and overlooks the *Golden Hinde*.

fish!,

Cathedral Street, SE1.
(020) 7234 3333.
Open: Mon–Sat 11.30–2.45, 5.30–10.30; Sun 12–3.30.
Main course: £9–16.

Chaotic canteen serving every kind of fish and seafood cooked as you like it in a trendy conservatory beside Borough Market.

BOROUGH MARKET

Borough High Street, SE10.
www.londonslarder.org.uk.
Open: Fri 12–6, Sat 9–4.
Transport: tube or train to London Bridge.

These days, Borough's 900-year-old market caters to the general public as well as the restaurant trade with a fantastic array of speciality foods from all over Europe, including wild mushrooms, hand-reared pork, Dorset scallops, organic beer, fresh game and poultry, quails' eggs and premium quality Melton Mowbray pork pies.

THE MONUMENT

Monument Street, EC3.
(020) 7626 2717.
Open: daily 10–5.40.
Admission: £1.50, 5s-15s 50p.
Transport: tube to Monument.

As you approach London Bridge, look out for the golden flames atop The Monument, a slim free-standing column commemorating the Great Fire of London. Designed in 1677 by Robert Hooke, it is 202ft tall and stands 202ft east of the bakery in Pudding Lane where the fire broke out on 2 September 1666. 'Psh! A woman might piss it out!' the Mayor of London exclaimed at the time, but the fire blazed for three days, destroying four-fifths of the City and displacing 100,000 Londoners. Nowadays, visitors who manage to climb the 311 steps to the top are awarded a fitness certificate.

LONDON BRIDGE

'London Bridge is falling down,' is putting it mildly. London's only river crossing from Roman times until the 18th century has fallen down eight times, most spectacularly in 1014 when the Vikings tied ropes around the supporting posts and rowed with all their might till it collapsed. A stone bridge with 19 arches was built in 1176 and, like the Ponte Vecchio in Florence, was crammed with shops, houses and even a chapel. Grisly looking spikes at either end displayed the heads of executed traitors, including the Scots patriot William 'Mel Gibson' Wallace, the English rebel Jack Cade, and Sir Thomas More. Holbein and Hogarth both had lodgings on the bridge, but in the 1750s the shops and houses were demolished and in 1831 a new London Bridge took its place. When this, too, showed signs of giving way, it was sold for $2.4 million (much to the amazement of the British, who assumed the buyer had mistaken it for Tower Bridge) to an American steel magnate who transported all 33,000 tons of it in 10,000 pieces to Havasu City, Arizona, where it was re-erected over a lake. An unexciting new bridge (pictured here) was built across the river in 1973.

THE OLD OPERATING THEATRE, MUSEUM & HERB GARRET

9a St Thomas' Street, SE1,
(020) 7955 4791.
Open: Tue-Sun 10-4 and most Mons.
Admission: £2.90, concs £1.50-2, family ticket £7.25.
Transport: riverboat to London Bridge City Pier; tube or train to London Bridge.

This mind-boggling time capsule was discovered by accident in 1957 when historian Raymond Russell squeezed through a hole in the belfry of a chapel belonging to old St Thomas' Hospital and discovered a pristinely preserved operating theatre in the garret room above. During the period that the operating theatre was in use anaesthetics and antiseptic surgery were unknown: amputations typically lasted 60 seconds or less and patients had to be doped up on ale or opiates and held down by assistants before the surgeons could get to work. The extraordinary museum, with its original blood-spattered floor and mop and bucket, includes a unique collection of surgical instruments and a medieval herb garret, used by the hospital's apothecary to make up medicinal compounds.

THE LONDON DUNGEON

28 Tooley St, SE1.
(020) 7403 7221.
www.dungeons.com
Open: Apr–Sept, daily 10–5.30; Oct–March, daily 10–5.
Admission: £9.95, concs £8.50, 4s-14s £6.50, wheelchair users free.
Transport: riverboat to London Bridge City Pier; tube or train to London Bridge.

This gorified haunted house contains an awesome range of high-decibel low-octane schlock-horror rides including the 'Jack the Ripper Experience', 'Madame Guillotine' and 'Judgment Day'. Fortunately, none are overly authentic.

FOOD AND DRINK

Café Rouge

Hay's Galleria, Tooley Street, SE1.
(020) 7378 0097.
Open: Mon–Fri 12–10pm; Sat–Sun 12–6pm.
Main course: £7–14.

Quality brasserie food (steak-frites, Caesar salad etc).

Kwan Thai

The Riverfront, Hay's Galleria, Tooley Street, SE1.
(020) 7403 7373.
Open: Mon–Fri 11.30–3, 6–10; Sat 6–10.
Main course: £10–12; set lunch from £7.95, set dinner from £25.

Aromatic Thai food.

Balls Brothers

Hay's Galleria, Tooley Street, SE1.
(020) 7407 4301
www.ballsbrothers.co.uk.
Open: Mon–Fri 11.30-9.30 (bar); Mon–Fri 11.45-2.45, 6-9 (restaurant). .
Main course: £6-£17.

Superior wine bar and speciality seafood restaurant.

OLD BILLINGSGATE FISH MARKET

This market sold fish from Saxon Times until the 1980s when Billingsgate was moved to the Isle of Dogs. With its distinctive gilded goldfish weather vanes, Billingsgate dates from 1875 and was designed by Horace Jones. Citibank took over the handsome building in 1982 when it was coverted, by Richard Rogers, into a securities dealing room

HAY'S GALLERIA

Built in 1860s, Thomas Cubitt's Hay's Wharf warehouses handled many kinds of goods, especially food. In 1988 the filled-in dock was converted into the ultimate retail-therapy heaven, a sleek shopping and eating galleria with a snaking glass roof and a plashing fountain and giant kinetic sculpture (by David Kemp) in the middle.

WINSTON CHURCHILL'S BRITAIN AT WAR EXPERIENCE

64 Tooley Street, SE1.
(020) 7403 3171.
www.britainatwar.co.uk
Open: Apr–Sept , daily 10–5.30; Oct–Mar, daily 10–4.30.
Admission: £5.95, 5s-16s £2.95, family ticket £14, concs £3.95.
Transport: riverboat to London Bridge City Pier; train or tube to London Bridge.

This museum takes a nostalgic look-back at London in the Blitz and has a real Anderson shelter, a reconstuctured tube station and lots of memorabilia.

HMS BELFAST

Morgan's Lane, Tooley Street, SE1.
(020) 7940 6328.
www.hmsbelfast.org.uk
Open: Mar–Oct, daily 10–6; Nov–Feb, daily 10–5.
Admission: £5, concs £3, free to under 16s.
Transport: riverboat to London Bridge City Pier; tube or train to
London Bridge.

With its blue and grey camouflage and tall, menacing gun turrets, the *Belfast* is an austerely beautiful piece of military hardware. Built in 1938, the 11,500-ton battle-cruiser saw active service from the outbreak of the Second World War until the end of the Korean War. Inside there are seven decks to explore, including boiler and engine rooms.

THE GREATER LONDON ASSEMBLY

Four hundred staff and Ken Livingstone – the ex-GLC leader elected Mayor of London in 2000 – are due to move into the brand new £20 million Greater London Assembly headquarters in 2001. The GLA succeeds the Greater London Council (abolished by Maggie Thatcher in 1986) and will oversee transport and economic planning in the metropolis, as well as the police. The glass building was designed by Norman Foster and will include a special jetty for visiting councillors, politicians and other dignatories.

TOWER OF LONDON

Tower Hill, EC3
(020) 7709 0765
Open: Mar–Oct, Mon–Sat 9–5, Sun 10–5; Nov–Feb, Tue–Sat 9–4,
Sun–Mon 10–4.
Admission: £9.50, concs £7.15, child £6.25
Transport: riverboat to Tower Millennium Pier; tube to Tower Hill.

William the Conqueror built three castles along the Thames after 1066. The first fortress on this site was made of wood, but over the next half century it was was rebuilt in white Normandy stone. With its 15ft-thick walls, the imposing tower was a mighty disincentive to aspiring English rebels.

In fact the Tower has never fallen. Monarchs have merely added to it, building tower after tower around the inner and outer walls of the original stronghold. In its time the Tower has housed a mint, arsenal, armoury, observatory, jewel house, lighthouse, records repository, bear-baiting arena and state prison. Henry III contributed a menagerie including elephants, leopards and a Norwegian polar bear, kept on a chain so it could fish on the river. These were joined by lions, eagles, mountain cats and a jackal until 1834, when one of the lions attacked a Beefeater and all the animals, except the ravens, were banished to London Zoo.

Most of the Tower's victims arrived by boat via Traitor's Gate, built originally for Edward I. As many as 1,000 traitors at a time were incarcerated inside, including Lady Jane Grey, Sir Thomas More, Bishop Fisher, Thomas Cromwell, Elizabeth I, the Earl of

Essex, Sir Walter Raleigh and Guy Fawkes. As late as 1914 the Irish nationalist Sir Roger Casement was shut up in the Tower before he was hanged for high treason, and in 1941 Rudolph Hess – Hitler's amanuensis and deputy Führer – was held here for four days.

The Tower is also, of course, home to 38 Yeoman Warders (nicknamed Beefeaters because of their 2lb daily meat rations) and the Crown Jewels. Cromwell sold off nearly all the royal jewellery in the Civil War and, except for three swords and an anointing spoon, all the treasures on display date from after 1660.

FOOD AND DRINK

The Hung, Drawn and Quartered

27 Great Tower Street, Tower Hill, EC3
(020) 7626 6123.
Food served: Mon–Sat 11–3, Sun 1–3.

An elegant Victorian bank, recently converted into a good pub.

TOWER BRIDGE

(020) 7403 3761
www.towerbridge.org.uk
Open: Apr-Oct, daily 10-6.30; Nov-Mar, daily 9.30-6.
Admission: £6.25, concs and 5s-15s £4.25, family ticket £18.25.
Transport: riverboat to Tower Millennium Pier; train/tube to London Bridge.

The great galumphing bridge was built by two men, John Wolfe-Barry and Horace Jones. Jones designed the jolly mock-medieval stone exterior; Barry was the brains behind the steel framework and the arms, or bascules, that rise into the air to let tall ships pass below. The two arms, weighing 1,000 tonnes each, were originally lifted by steam engines in the south-side tower. In its first year (1894–5) the arms were raised as often as 16 times a day. River freight traffic has declined since then, but Tower Bridge is still raised at least once a day, mostly for tourist cruise boats (020 7378 7700 to find out when).

Admission includes entrance to the the original steam engine rooms, the high-level walkways for pedestrians and the Tower Bridge Experience, an engaging interactive exhibition about the bridge which includes an artist's impression of the audacious London bus which managed to get up speed and leap across the opening as the bascules were rising.

ST KATHARINE'S DOCK

There were protests in Parliament when St Katharine's Dock was built in 1828, but the excavations went ahead and in the space of one month 1,250 houses including a 12th-century church and hospital were demolished and 11,000 people were rendered homeless. In their place a sleek complex of warehouses with arcades by Thomas Telford and Philip Hardwick was built around the basin and used for storing wine, rum, dried fruit, dried flowers, tea, wool, ivory and indigo. Though only small, the docks could handle up to 1,000 ships and 10,000 lighters (the flat-bottomed craft used for unloading ships).

St Katherine's closed in 1968 and was one of the first of London's docks to be redeveloped with shops, cafés and pubs, and a central yachting marina. David Mellor, lives in the Harbour Master's house overlooking the dock and records his regular Sunday Classic FM radio programme from the premises.

BUTLER'S WHARF

From the early 19th century onwards Butler's Wharf was one of London's busiest trading docks for tea, coffee, spices, rubber, spirit, grain and flour. The warehouses were renovated by Terence Conran in the 1980s and now, beneath 98 luxury flats, the wharf harbours a speciality wine and food mall (charcuterie, smoked fish, crustacea, bagels), plus a Conran restaurantopolis comprising the Pont de la Tour, Butler's Wharf Chop House and the Blue Print Café. In its prime Butler's Wharf handled up to 6,000 chests of tea a day and, at the back of the warehouses you can still see the aerial bridges used for bundling bags from building to building.

BRAMAH TEA & COFFEE MUSEUM
Gainsford Street, near Maguire Street, SE1
(020) 7378 0222
www.bramahmuseum.co.uk
Open: daily 10-6.
Admission: £4, concs and 5s-15s £3, family ticket £10.
Transport: riverboat to St Katherine's Pier; tube or train to London Bridge then P11, 15, 42, 47 or 78 bus.

This full fresh-flavoured museum was set up by the commodity broker and tea aficionado Edward Bramah. His amazing collection of over 1,000 tea and coffee pots tells the intricate story of tea and coffee, from the 17th century coffeehouses which spawned the Stock Exchange and Lloyds Insurance to that most elegiac of 20th century inventions, the mass-produced and fast-infusing tea bag. A more authentic brew is made in the museum's two cafés and the shop sells a choice selection of Assam, Ceylon and Darjeeling leaf-teas.

FOOD AND DRINK

Aquarium

Ivory House, St Katharine-by-the-Tower, E1
(020) 7480 6116.
Open: Mon–Sat 12–3, 6.30–11; Sun 12–3.
Main course: £14–23; set meals from £14.50.

Imaginative fish restaurant overlooking St Katharine's Dock.

Butler's Wharf Chophouse

Butler's Wharf Building, 36E Shad Thames, SE1
(020) 7403 3403.
Open: Mon–Sat 12–3, 6pm–11; Sun 12-3.–
Main course: £15–30 (restaurant), £7-20 (bar); set meals in the bar from £10
for three courses; or Sat–Sun set brunch from £13.95 for two courses.

British food – salmon fish cakes, saddle of lamb and roast beef - with lovely views of Tower Bridge from an outdoor terrace.

The Apprentice

Cardamon Building, 31 Shad Thames, SE1
(020) 7234 0254.
Open: Mon–Fri 12–1.30, 6.30–8.30.
Main course: £8–12.50; set lunch from £10.50; set dinner from £15.50.

Meals at this cut-price Conran restaurant are cooked by trainees from Butler's Wharf Chef School.

Le Pont de la Tour

Butler's Wharf Building, 36D Shad Thames, SE1
(020) 7403 8403
Open: Mon–Sat 11.30–11.30; Sun 12–11.
Main course: £20–30; Mon-Fri set lunch from £28.50; Mon-Sat set dinner from
£19.50 served from 6–6.45 and 10.45–11.30 only.

This is Conran's flagship restaurant, where lofty views of the river combine with astronomical prices.

Cantina del Ponte

Butler's Wharf Building, 36C Shad Thames, SE1
(020) 7403 5403
Open: Mon–Fri 12–3, 6–11; Sat 12–4, 6–11; Sun 12–4, 6–10.
Main course: average £10.

Classic Mediterranean food (pizza, piperade, zabaglione).

THE DESIGN MUSEUM

Butler's Wharf, Shad Thames, SE1
(020) 7403 6933
www.designmuseum.org
Open: daily 11.30–6 (last entry 5.30).
Admission: £5.50, students £4.50, other concs and 5s-15s £4, family ticket £15.
Transport: riverboat to St Katherine's Pier; tube or train to London Bridge then 15, 78 or 100 bus.

Created by Terence Conran and Stephen Bayley, the Design Museum is the only museum in the world devoted to industrial design and the cult of consumerism. A bower bird's shrine on the second floor showcases such mass production classics as the car (original designs by Le Corbusier from 1928), the vacuum (Dyson *et al*), early televisions and radios, telephones, tableware (by Enzo Mari) and chairs (by Charles and Ray Eames), while the ground floor is devoted to a diverse and diverting range of temporary exhibitions ranging from Bosch washing machines to the visionary designs of Isambard Kingdom Brunel. The museum is based in a disused warehouse which Conran and his partners rebuilt and, in a somewhat wistful homage to the International Style, painted white.

FOOD AND DRINK

Blue Print Café

Design Museum, Butler's Wharf, SE1
(020) 7378 7031
Open: Mon–Sat 12–2.45, 6–10.45; Sun 12–2.45.
Main course: £12–17.

The best of the Conran restaurants, this attractive Design Museum eaterie serves high quality if costly French and Italian food. Top-notch nosh, with an outdoor terrace and exquisite views.

WAPPING

In the 19th century Wapping seethed with seafarers, ship-makers, caulkers, rope- and mast-makers, and pirates. The East End novelist Arthur Morrison vividly evoked its scents and smells: 'something of tar, something of rope and junk, something of ships' stores, and much of a blend of unknown outlandish merchandise. We met sailors, some with parrots and accordions, and many with undecided legs...'

Oliver's Wharf, used for storing tea from India and China, was one of the first docklands warehouses to be converted into luxury flats in the 1970s and '80s. In 1986 Wapping was dubbed 'Fortress Wapping' after Rupert Murdoch incurred the wrath of printers and journalists alike when in a single night he disgorged *The Times*, the *Sunday Times*, the *Sun* and the *News of the World* into non-union computerised printing works on Wapping High Street.

FOOD AND DRINK

Town of Ramsgate

62 Wapping High Street, E1
(020) 7264 0001
Food served: Mon–Fri 12–3, 6–8; Sat 12–6; Sun 12-4–
Transport: tube to Wapping.

The legendary Wapping pub where 'hanging Judge Jeffreys' got his comeuppance in 1688. Nowadays the pub is renowned for its filthy rugby songs (Dinah, Dinah, show us yer legs, etc).

The Angel

101 Bermondsey Wall East, Rotherhithe, SE16
(020) 7237 3608
Food served: Mon–Fri 12–1.45, 7–9.30, Sat 7–9.30, Sun 12.30–2.30.
Transport: tube to Rotherhithe.

There are spectacular views of Tower Bridge from this venerable sailors' pub on the south side of the river in Bermondsey.

THE THAMES TUNNEL &
BRUNEL'S ENGINE HOUSE

The only sign above ground of the world's first underwater tunnel is the tall iron chimney of the engine house built by Marc Brunel to drain the excavations of pulp and water. The tunnel took 20 years and thousands of pounds to build, and a catalogue of disasters, human, financial and natural, beset the engineering wonder along the way. Water burst through at least five times, drowning men whose colleagues had already died or been blinded by 'tunnel sickness' (in one of the floods Brunel's son, Isambard, dived in and saved a miner). When it opened in 1843 the underwater tunnel became a tourist attraction; glassblowers and stalls selling cakes and ginger beer set up inside and a million people paid a penny entrance fee to walk beneath the Thames. In the 1860s the first tracks were laid down for trains, and tubes from Rotherhithe to Wapping hurtle through the tunnel to this day.

FOOD AND DRINK

Prospect of Whitby

57 Wapping Wall, E1
(020) 7481 1095
Food served: Mon–Sat 12–2.30 and 6–9, Sun 12–3 and 6–9.

Dating from 1520, The Prospect of Whitby is one of London's oldest and most atmospheric river pubs. Originally named the Devil's Tavern, it was a notorious criminals' and smugglers' hide-out.

The Grapes

76 Narrow Street, E14
(020) 7987 4396
Food served: daily 7–9, Mon–Fri 12–2, Sun 12–3.
Transport: DLR to Limehouse.

With a verandah overlooking the Thames and an interior dating from 1619, The Grapes is one of London's most authentic river pubs. The first floor has a first-class fish restaurant.

LIMEHOUSE MARINA

Limehouse was named after the lime kilns built here in medieval times and fired as recently as 1935. The lime was made from chalk brought by river from Kent and was used in the building trade for mixing into sand and cement to make mortar.

In the 19th century 300 Chinese sailors and dockworkers moved into the area and Limehouse evolved into a shipbuilding hub. Its narrow streets and alleyways, bursting with brothels and gaming houses, became a virtual no-go area for the police, and in Victorian fiction the area became a byword for iniquity and vice. Dorian Gray ventured into Limehouse to look for opium dens in Wilde's The *Picture of Dorian Gray*, Dickens used it as the setting for the Six Jolly Fellowship Porters ('a tavern of dropsical appearance') in Our Mutual Friend, and it frequently cropped up in the detective stories of Conan Doyle and Sax Rohmer's Fu Manchu.

In recent years Limehouse has been gentrified with yachting marinas and luxury redevelopments, but a few Chinese residents remain and the area is renowned for its Chinese restaurants. Limehouse Basin, just beyond Limehouse Marina, connects to Regent's Canal and, ultimately, to Birmingham. St Anne's Limehouse was built in 1724 and is one of Hawksmoor's most exquisite and unusual churches. Its stark white tower and pointed turrets are still a landmark for shipping sailing into London.

CANARY WHARF & THE ISLE OF DOGS

At 812ft Canary Wharf is the tallest building in the UK (and the second tallest in Europe). It towers over the rest of London and it winks at onlookers. The novelist Iain Sinclair called it 'that blunt acupuncture needle, that dissatisfied glass erection ...', and for Londoners, too, Canary Wharf and its surrounding canyons of office buildings and plastic housing developments seem more like an alien encampment than any recognisable part of London. The tower was built in 1991 by the Canadian property developers Olympia & York; it took £4 billion and 18 months to construct and was the first skyscraper in the world to be clad in stainless steel. But as recession tightened tenants were slow to come forward, and Olympia & York, haemorrhaging money at the rate of £38 million a day, went bankrupt within the year. More disaster struck, four years later in February 1996, when an IRA bomb blew up near Sugar Quay, killing two people and destroying a million square foot of office space. In recent years the tower's fortunes have turned around and it is now fully occupied by such high profile organisations as the *Independent*, the *Daily Telegraph* and The Bank of New York. Two new enormous office blocks are being built nearby and it is estimated that, on their completion in 2006, Canary Wharf will absorb up to 100,000 office workers a day.

In the 19th century Canary Wharf was the main recipient of banana cargoes from the Canary Islands. The connection with dogs is more nebulous: most probably it is a corruption of dykes (a network of dykes and windmills were built across it in the 17th century to stop the marshes flooding) – though legend has it that the royal kennels were kept on the Isle of Dogs so that monarchs sleeping in Greenwich would not hear them barking.

CUTTY SARK
King William Walk, SE10
(020) 8858 344
www.cuttysark.org.uk
Open: daily 10—5.
Admission: £3.50, concs and 5s-15s £2.50; combined ticket to National Maritime Museum and Royal Observatory £12, concs £9.60, under 16s £2.50.
Transport: riverboat to Greenwich Pier; DLR to Cutty Sark.

The last of the great tea clippers, the *Cutty Sark* was also the speediest. Launched in Scotland in 1869, she was specially designed for racing, and in 1871 she won the annual clippers' race from Shanghai to London, completing the voyage in a record 107 days. For the next two decades the ship brought tea from India and China and wool and grain from Australia. The clipper is named after the 'cutty sark' or short chemise worn by its figurehead and inspired by the witch called Nellie who wears a 'cutty sark' (a corruption of the French 'courte chemise') in Burns' great poem *Tam O'Shanter*.

FOOD AND DRINK

The Gipsy Moth

60 Greenwich Church Street, SE10
(020) 8858 0786.
Food served: daily 12-3.

Good pub, near the Cutty Sark.

GREENWICH FOOT TUNNEL

The glass-topped domes either side of the river are entrances to an underwater tunnel for pedestrians which was built in 1902–3 and connects Greenwich to the Isle of Dogs and Docklands DLR (walking through it takes about five minutes).

FOOD AND DRINK

Goddards Pie and Mash Shop

21 Greenwich Church Street, SE10
(020) 8692 3601.
Open: Mon–Fri, 9.30–4.

Established in 1890, Goddard's is the place to go for proper East End pie and mash with 'liquor' (the fluorescent green stuff made from whizzed up parsley).

THE OLD ROYAL NAVAL COLLEGE

King William Walk, SE10
(020) 8269 4744
www.greenwichfoundation.org.uk
Open: Mon–Sat 10–5, Sun 12.30–5.
Admission: £5, concs £3, under 16s free (accompanied by adult).
Transport: riverboat to Greenwich Pier; DLR to Cutty Sark.

The opening scenes of Harrison Ford's Patriot Games were

filmed along the Royal Naval College's handsome Thames facade and Greenwich itself, with its photogenic buildings, park and market, is often used for film and tv shoots. Built on the site of Henry VIII's pleasure palace (Placentia), the Naval College was originally a hospital for disabled sailors, commissioned in 1696 and the combined work of three great architects – Wren, Hawksmoor and Vanbrugh. In 1998 the Royal Navy moved out and the college became home to the University of Greenwich.

THE QUEEN'S HOUSE
Romney Road, SE10
(020) 8858 4422
recorded info (020) 8312 6565
Open: daily 10–5.
Admission: £7.50, concs £6, 5s-15s £3.75.
Transport: riverboat to Greenwich Pier; DLR to Cutty Sark.

Set between two wings of the Royal Naval College, the

Queen's House was built for Anne of Denmark in 1615. The architect was Inigo Jones, who had just visited Venice and was inspired by his trip to build a palace modelled on the villa designs of Palladio. The simple classical exterior contrasts with a sumptuous interior decorated with paintings by Titian, Rubens, Raphael, Gentileschi (who did the ceilings) and Van Dyck.

THE NATIONAL MARITIME MUSEUM

Romney Road, SE10
(020) 8858 4422
recorded info (020) 8312 6565
www.nmm.ac.uk
Open: daily 10–5.
Admission: £7.50, concs £6, 5s-15s £3.75; combined ticket to Cutty Sark and Royal Observatory £12, concs £9.60, under 16s £2.50.
Transport: riverboat to Greenwich Pier; DLR to Cutty Sark.

The imaginatively revamped National Maritime Museum charts every aspect of the sea, maritime history and the importance of the oceans in our lives today. Highlights for children include the largest paper boat in the world and 'All Hands', an interactive box of delights where kids can steer a Viking ship using sails, oars and rudder, or manoeuvre a Sea Cat high speed ferry out of Dover Harbour. For older visitors 'Exploration' traces the history of sea exploration from pre-history to the discovery of 1,000m deep lake in Antarctica in 1997. The contentious 'Empire and Trade' focuses on the dark side of the British Empire, while 'Maritime' London analyses of the role of shipping in the creation of the City. Other highlights include the gilded barge decorated with mermaids and dolphins built for the Prince of Wales in 1732, the Nelson rooms which feature a computer animated Battle of Trafalgar by Jim Henson and such evocative memorabilia as the tourniquet worn by Nelson after his right arm was amputated and the bullet-punctured uniform in which he died at Trafalgar.

THE ROYAL OBSERVATORY & PLANETARIUM
Romney Road, SE10
(020) 8858 4422
recorded info (020) 8312 6565
Open: daily 10–5.
Admission: £6, concs £4.80, under 16s free; combined ticket to Cutty Sark and Maritime Museum £12, concs £9.60, under 16s £2.50.
Transport: riverboat to Greenwich Pier; DLR to Cutty Sark.

Here at 0° longitude east and western hemispheres collide and visitors can straddle the Prime Meridian line with a foot in either time zone. Designed by Christopher Wren in 1675, the Observatory was set up to find a way to measure longitude, a problem which was solved eventually a century later by a carpenter from Yorkshire. John Harrison built his first marine clock in 1730 and spent his life working on four more prototypes. He finally found a solution in 1772, aged 79, and even then it was only after George III intervened on his behalf that he was awarded the £20,000 prize money offered by a 1714 Act of Parliament. The Observatory tells Harrison's compelling story with the help of various navigational instruments including the 13ft pendulum which Harrison used to measure the rotation of the earth.

FOOD AND DRINK

Trafalgar Tavern
Park Row, SE10
(020) 8858 2437
Food served: Tues-Sat 12pm-10pm, Mon-Sun 12-3.

This grand old riverside pub commemorates the Battle of Trafalgar. In the 19th century the Trafalgar was famous for its whitebait and champagne suppers: Dickens used it as a setting for the wedding feast in *Our Mutual Friend*, and real life visitors included Wagner, Gladstone and a distinguished line of senior Liberal MPs who gathered at the tavern every Sunday after Whitsun (Tory MPs patronised another Greenwich pub, The Ship). The Trafalgar reopened after 50 years in 1965 and still serves whitebait suppers.

TRINITY HOSPITAL ALMSHOUSES

This miniature castle dates from 1613 and is Greenwich's oldest building. The almshouses, with their private chapel and gardens, are run by a City livery company and house about 20 pensioners. One of their most treasured possessions is a collection of mummified rats dating from the 1665 Great Plague, when thousands of Londoners took refuge in ships near Greenwich: 'I could not but applaud the contrivance,' Daniel Defoe wrote in his *Journal of the Plague Year*, 'ten thousand people, and more... sheltered here from the violence of the contagion, and lived very safe and easy.'

GREENWICH SILOS

The four silos in this riverside factory are filled with maize and corn used for processing into cooking oil, custard powder, vodka and gin.

REUTERS' BUILDING

Designed in 1989 by Richard Rogers of Pompidou fame, this sullen looking building is the headquarters of the London branch of Reuters, the global news agency which began in 1849 as a continental pigeon post. In a celebration of the aesthetics of Meccano, the exterior is emblazoned with cranes, lift shafts, bits of pierced metal, satellite dishes and other macho hardware.

THE MILLENNIUM DOME

As horrid to behold and as difficult to get rid of as a gigantic semi-sebaceous cyst, the Dome will go down as a ministerial cock-up of appropriately millennial proportions. Ineptitude and incompetence dogged the project from the start: one month after it opened it went bankrupt; several massive cash injections later it failed to attract even half the 12m people originally predicted. By December 31 2000 the Dome had cost the nation nearly a billion pounds, £628m of which had been paid for, by the public, directly out of National Lottery funds (at a total cost of approximately £150 per visitor).

In November 2000, the saga took a bizarre twist when four incompetent robbers wearing gas masks charged into the Dome astride a JCB bulldozer and, dashing fences to the ground and casting smokebombs in their wake, tried to steal a 203-carat diamond worth £350m from a concrete vault inside the Money Zone. Police–who had been tipped off months before—were lying in wait for them disguised as cleaners. As with the rocket missile attack on Vauxhall Cross, aspects of the heist emulated scenes from the Bond film The World is Not Enough which climaxed with a speedboat chase and showdown at the Dome. As fact followed fiction so fiction has followed fact, and a BBC drama is already in the pipeline.

Yet more controversy has surrounded the proposed sale of the Dome to property developers Legacy for £125m, when it was known all along that demolishing the Richard Rogers-designed structure and selling the site only would fetch in the region of £300m. If the sale goes ahead, Legacy plan to turn the Dome into a science park called Knowledge City for IT, e-commerce and bio-science related businesses.

THE MILLENNIUM VILLAGE

Providing housing for up to 7,500 residents along a 2.2km riverside boulevard, the £250m Millennium Village is being developed on a polluted gasworks site on Greenwich peninsula. Work on the troubled brownfield project is years behind schedule and, in 1999, the lead architects resigned complaining that their original vision, of a sustainable community which integrated luxury and affordable housing, had been watered down by the developers who were segregating cheaper residences on the least attractive plots.

BIRDLIFE

The timber cross-pieces pictured here came from an 1870s jetty and were recycled as perches for ducks, herring gulls, terns, herons and cormorants fishing in the river and also to provide algae below the water for shrimps and mullet. New reed beds are also being planted on river-walls to tempt back creatures scared away when building works on the Dome began.

THAMES BARRIER

1 Unity Way, SE18
(020) 8305 4188
www.environment-agency.gov.uk.
Open: Mon–Fri 10–5, Sat–Sun 10.30–5.30.
Admission: £3.40, concs and 5s-16s £2, family ticket £7.50.
Transport: riverboat to Barrier Gardens Pier.

The Thames Barrier makes a fitting terminus to this vital stretch of the Thames. Beneath its ten majestic silver-steel hoods the barrier's gates span 520 metres of river, protecting a million Londoners from floods caused by a mixture of tidal surges from Canada, global warming and geological forces which are upending Britain into the southeast coast by 1ft every 100 years.

In 1953 a committee chaired by John Anderson (inventor of the air-raid shelter) was set up to deal with the rising water problem after floods deluged the England's east coast, drowning 300 people and decimating farmland. Inspired by his observations of the household gas-tap, an engineer called Charles Draper came up with a design for a barrier

with rotating gates. In normal conditions the gates lie flat on the riverbed on concrete sills. In a flood, the yellow hydraulic arms attached to the stainless steel hoods rotate the gates through 90° to form a 66ft high wall. The gates are manned 24 hours a day and can be raised, at the push of a button, in ten minutes. They have gone up 35 times since the Barrier opened in 1984 (the only collision occurring in 1998 when a dredger carrying 3,300 tonnes of sand and gravel collided into one of the gates and sank between piers 4 and 5). With sea levels rising 2ft every century the Barrier's usefulness will come to an end in 2030.

TATE & LYLE THAMES REFINERY

For most of the 19th century sugar was produced in loaves which grocers had to break up into pieces. But in the 1880s, after Henry Tate purchased the license to a method patented by Eugen Langen (a German entrepreneur and the inventor of the suspension railway), sugar began to be produced in cubes at this Thameside refinery.

Sugar cubes made Tate's fortune: he moved into a mansion in Streatham and started to collect Pre-Raphaelite art. But Tate was the seventh son of a Unitarian minister from Lancashire and, as well as making money, he gave vast sums of it away. Many of the schools, libraries and hospitals still in use in South London and Liverpool today were the fruits of his philanthropy. In 1890, urged on by his second wife, he founded the Tate Gallery, a national gallery of British art which he endowed with works from his own collection by Millais, J. M. Waterhouse, Luke Fildes and Alma Tadema. Tate died in 1899 and, in 1921, the company merged with Lyle & Sons, whose golden syrup factory was a mile and a half downriver in Plaistow. Tate & Lyle are now a

multinational concern with interests in 50 countries in Africa, Asia, Australia and the Americas (where Tate owns Domino Sugar, the leading table-top brand).

The planes landing and taking off behind the refinery come from London City Airport. Beyond the Thames Refinery and Silvertown the Thames Estuary slowly widens until it opens out into the colder waters of the North Sea and the Dover Strait.